Kingdom P

# GOD'S KINGDOM AND OUR CULTURES IN GENESIS

*The Beginnings of God's Gospel Dream*

Dr. Larry L. Niemeyer

*Original – 1999*
*Revised edition - 2013*



*ISBN-10: 1490978127*
*ISBN-13: 9781490978123*

# DEDICATION

This book is affectionately dedicated to the memory of Albert and Elsie Niemeyer, parents who stood with us through the thick and thin of the first 32 years of our mission work. I liked to call them "Shoulders and Teardrops" for two of the most endearing qualities of their lives–strength and love.

*Shoulders,*
*broad and strong*
*pedestals on which I stand*
*seeing visions long*
*–far promised land.*

*Teardrops,*
*soft and silent*
*streams in which I move*
*following visions sent*
*–land to prove.*

# ACKNOWLEDGMENTS

Many people have taken part in the writing of this book. Three hundred prayer partners prayed with me during the final four years. Former students kept the desire burning as they asked about progress. Friends and colleagues read so many different versions, they will ponder the finished product and ask if it resembles what they remember. Family members humbly yielded to time and economic necessities.

The one person who really made this book possible, however, is the late Mrs. Connie Soth, my "book doctor." Tireless editing, challenging improvements, friendly encouragement, patient endurance–all these with an extra measure of God's love and grace leave an indelible gratefulness in my heart.

Who would have known that a young teenager knocking on her door in the 1950s to say, "Collecting for the Oregon Journal," would knock on that door again forty years later asking for help in writing a vision. What a special relationship, what a grand experience. Thank you, Connie.

# CONTENTS

# FIGURES

# TABLE

# PREFACE TO THE FIRST EDITION

Needed today is . . .

> the "recovery of forgotten first things."
> a "re-ordering of life priorities in our cultures"
> the recognition of shifting perspectives
> a rethinking of our Christian identities
> the reformation of our thought,
> even the revision of our faith.

So goes the advice of many astute observers of our contemporary times.

How do God's people respond to such challenges? Familiarity with the first things of other people along with their different life priorities, perspectives and identities only compounds the challenge. What impact does the observation of shifting perspectives have upon our understanding of global issues? When other writers claim that the search for a defining center is urgent if Christians are to engage cultures with a coherent gospel, how shall we respond when they themselves fail to develop vibrant, all-encompassing frameworks? How adequate are the "new visions beyond yesterday's images" they foster, the new ventures they recommend in order to break from our frenzied activity hurtling in all directions?

The challenge drives thoughtful believers to Genesis–a divinely appropriate place to begin the recovery, revision and reformation. Genesis reminds us of the futility of endlessly inventing new identities when a deeply profound one still awaits our discovery. A life-defining center as well as a dynamic, all-encompassing circumference explode from this first book of the Bible, making it clear that the desired new vision and venture is actually more than merely ancient.

This study, appropriate to individuals or groups, can revive heavenly expectations, renew vision. Genesis has the power to reshape our lives by leading us to probe the on-going encounter between God's Kingdom plans for us and our own self-centered cultural designs. When our lives engage with the LIFE of God as he has always intended, there emerges an unshakable hope for transcendent ideas and life-changing actions in our chaotic times.

# PREFACE TO THE SECOND EDITION

This second editionreplaces the original edition called Kingdom and Culture in Genesis. It also re-names the series to "A Kingdom Perspective on Global Issues," instead of "A Kingdom Perspective on Mission." The first audience had been Christian mission personnel. The new audience includesall Christians interested in today's international concerns such as religion, poverty, politics, economy, education, human rights, and freedom. The global issues also relate to personal families, groups, the communities we live in, our nations, and the world at large.

This edition highlights reference to God's LIFE from the very beginning of the book. His LIFE is always distinguished from human life by the use of capital letters. That LIFE is consistently connected to God's eternal Kingdom plan and more deliberatelycontrasts with human life connected to our cultural plans.

Finally, this edition has been re-written after fourteen years whenadditional writing clarified the original intent. A complete 38-book college curriculum was created highlighting the contents of the original book and showing their practicality for Christian living. The design of that curriculum included a comprehensive study of the entire Bible from a Kingdom perspective and showing the LIFE-in-life gospel from Genesis to Revelation. It also traced the conflict between God's Kingdom and the cultures of men from Genesis to Revelation. Because of those efforts, the sub-title for this edition is no longer "When LIFE Meets Life," but "The Beginnings of God's Gospel Dream."

Two additional books were also written during those fourteen years. The LIFE-in-life gospel was put forward more boldly for evangelism and discipleship. The reception given God's Dream: A Refreshing Look at the Gospel and Dream-walking: The Sacred Dimension of Discipleship made me realize that readers needed to see the extent to which one can go at implementing a comprehensive Kingdom perspective on everything about life everywhere in the world. That's what this new edition attempts to do.

# INTRODUCTION

## TODAY'S KALEIDOSCOPE OF CULTURES AND ETERNITY'S KINGDOM

A few years back, before the colorful world of television, computer, and constant media changes, a small device called the kaleidoscope entertained our eyes and minds with artistic patterns of glorious colors.[1]This small tube, a toy about eight inches long and two inches in diameter had a small hole at one end through which to see these designs. Invented in the early 1800s, the kaleidoscope operated by means of two mirrors inside the tube and two covers on either end, one made of ground glass and the other clear. The mirrors reflected small colored pieces of glass deposited between the ends while the rough edges of the ground glass cover threw the light in unexpected directions as we turned the kaleidoscope in our hands. Intricate patterns appeared opposite the peep hole–especially when pointed toward the sun.

What could a kaleidoscope teach us?

In the 1990s this toy came to relate to my life-long study of cultures, defined as human patterns of living in different environments. Consider the tube as it confines the various elements of the kaleidoscope. Cultural patterns, too, are contained within a limited environment. Earthly conditions impose boundaries affecting our designs for living. Flora, fauna, climate and terrain influence the way people survive. A desert environment is not as hospitable to large wooden houses as a forest climate would be. High altitude lifestyles differ markedly from low altitude ways of living.

Consider the colored pieces of glass. These compare to the elements making up a single pattern for living–a single culture–in a given place. Some pieces represent religious, social and economic values. Other fragments depict beliefs. Still other colored portions characterize the authority of family and institutions. Norms of behavior provide more shapes and colors. Together, they create a single pattern, a culture, which could be American, African, Asian, European or Latin in nature.

A North American plan, for example, often highlights freedom, individuality, information, choice, equality and self-reliance. These tinted fragments of glass in a special environment give America a distinct design for living. Homes, churches, institutions, companies and cities reflect the design. In Africa, my second home for 47 years, the kaleidoscope highlights security, community, power, unity and control. These elements, like different hues, shapes and angles, give Africa distinct cultural patterns unlike those of America. For example, in the constant changes characteristic of this continent, a person may be more concerned for security than for freedom, the government for community and power than for individuality and information. Unity and control often take precedence over equality and self-reliance in Africa.

Consider the kaleidoscopic nature of today's plurality–colorful, complex, and ever-changing. Elements and ingredients unite in diverse ways and people living amidst the elements multiply the complexity. The environment or "tube" never remains stationary as forces within and without continually shift pluralistic patterns to brilliant new designs. People, values, beliefs, and knowledge seem to change with a shake of the hand. Patterns for living, once framed and fixed in a slower pace of life are now fragmented and fleeting in these bewildering times.

These patterns resemble kaleidoscopic designs in a still more remarkable way. The toy offers no visual adventure if looked at in a dark room. Only in the light can intricate designs be seen. Cultures, too, need a light to illuminate and define their colors, lines and substance. I believe that light to be God's LIFE and his Kingdom plan, his design streams through every crack, glows behind every obstruction. As John described Jesus at the beginning of his gospel, *"In him was LIFE, and that LIFE was the light of all mankind."*[2] While patterns of living embrace the darkness to ease conformity, God's Kingdom based upon his LIFE keeps putting holes in that darkness, revealing LIFE beyond our plans and protective walls, daring us to be transformed people of God. Except for that light, there would be no design, no brilliance, no creativity, nothing to see–darkness.

Dazzled by the designs of a kaleidoscope, we often overlook the source of the light. Dazzled by culture and its life we often overlook the significant illumination of God's LIFE in Kingdom light. We see this with the coming of Christ as reported by John: *"In him was life, and that life was the light of men. The light shines in the darkness, but the darkness has not understood it."*[3] The people of his day obscured his presence by the shadows and reflections of their cultures. Yet his light continued to radiate the Kingdom: *"When Jesus spoke again to the people, he said, 'I am the light of the world. Whoever follows me will never walk in darkness, but will have the light of life'".*[4] Peter, too, finally saw beyond life-centered human patterns to the light of LIFE shining behind them: *"But you are a chosen people, a royal priesthood, a holy nation, a people belonging to God, that you may declare the praises of him who called you out of darkness into his wonderful light".*[5]

Here is a book about life-centered cultural plans and the LIFE-centered Kingdom plan of God, the contrast and conflict between human patterns for living and God's own grand design. Realizing the designs flashing across our international experience, we can revel in God's eternal plan permitting us to see. The investigation centers upon the opening pages of Genesis. Chapters 1-2 lay the foundation for our study, chapters 3-5 link the Kingdom to the first two chapters of Genesis and Chapters 6-9 show the contrast of God's Kingdom plan and our cultural plans. Chapters 10-12 discuss the application of the perspective as the gospel of Genesis leads to Kingdom action in our chaotic times. Bound to our diverse human heritage in cultures, we are divinely blessed by a common destiny in the Kingdom. The intermingling of these two plans for living is what Kingdom and Culture in Genesis is about.

## Part I

# FOUNDATIONS FOR KINGDOM APPROACHES TO GLOBAL ISSUES

Chapter 1

# THE OTHER SIDE OF OUR BEGINNING

"In the beginning"–those first three words of the Bible have always tantalized readers. Knowing how consumed we would be with questions of time, God certainly knew how to get our attention. Unfortunately, we usually focus only to one side of the beginning. We have rightly considered events since the beginning, but we have failed to see that they echo or resonate from what existed before the beginning.

## WHAT HAPPENED BEFORE TIME?

When we look at the moon, we don't see its immediate appearance but as it was one second ago. The sun looked at now is not the sun of the present but the sun of eight minutes ago. The nearest star to our eyes is a star of four years ago. Why? Light travels at a specified speed and these are the times required for these sights to reach us. When telescopes show us stars beyond the nearest ones, we are seeing much further back in time. Secular astronomers say light from distant galaxies, super novas and quasars have traveled for billions of years.[6] To deal with the incongruities of such thinking, a limerick made the rounds in the 1960s:

There once was a lady named Bright
Who could travel faster than light
She went out one day
In a relative way
And came back the previous night.

Stephen Hawking, brilliant astrophysicist of the 90s has observed that the time evident in the stars must have a beginning.[7] Hugh Ross, a Christian in the same profession, declares that "a minimum of nine dimensions of space and time were somehow involved in our beginnings."[8] Brilliant minds explore time and our origins. Their remarkable discoveries and proposals lead to a question of even more significance: "What happened before time?"

Like many other Christians, I always began my study of these subjects by going to Genesis: "In the beginning . . .." One day when comparing three Scriptures in the New International Version of the Bible, I was struck by their emphasis on one point. First, Paul, writing to Timothy, says,

> . . . join with me in suffering for the gospel, by the power of God, who has saved us and called us to a holy life . . . because of his purpose and grace. This grace was given us in Christ Jesus *before the beginning of time.*[9]

Then, writing to Titus, he says,

> . . . for the faith of God's elect and the knowledge of the truth that leads to godliness . . . a faith and knowledge resting on the hope of eternal life, which God, who does not lie, *promised before the beginning of time . . ..*[10]

And, Peter, writing to scattered Christians, says,

> He (Christ) was *chosen before the creation of the world*, but was revealed in these last times for your sake.[11]

These, together with the Lord's testimony in John 17, provide rich food for thought. Jesus said, "And now, Father, glorify me in your presence with the glory I had with you *before the world began*".[12] Later he added, "Father, I want those you have given me to be with me where I am, and to see my glory, the glory you have given me because *you loved me before the creation of the world.*"

## WHAT PRECEDED GENESIS?

The repetition of the adverb "*before*" in significant scriptures caused me to probe *before* Genesis to discover events preceding our beginnings. Other scriptures lent remarkable content to this curious yet obscure word in God's revelation:

- Before the foundation of the world, God's wisdom and grace foresaw the salvation of people.[13]

- He appointed us to be his children, to have life, to be included in the book of life.[14]
- He envisioned the Church.[15]
- He prepared the Kingdom experience for those who would be its citizens.[16]
- He appointed his Son to be his means of creating, ruling, preserving, saving, and finally judging all creation.[17]

Before Genesis, an eternal, loving plan radiates from God himself. Shining more brilliantly than the sun, this plan warmly glows behind all the events of time. We think of time in the past, present or future tense, attributing origins and endings. Within this framework, the topic of "beginnings" applies. Before this framework, however, there exists another–the light of Eternity. The writer of Ecclesiastes saw the gentleness of this prior radiance behind events when he wrote, "He has made everything beautiful in its time".[18] Eternity gives substance to time, standing in ultimate reality beyond time, embracing all time frames but being confined to none, existing before the beginning and enduring beyond the end.

Most importantly, Eternity stretches our lives beyond our familiar time frames. The writer of Ecclesiastes continues in 3:11,

"He has also set Eternity in the hearts of men . . .."

Even a skeptical astrophysicist like Stephen Hawking is challenged by the possibilities. Christians, too, struggle with the concept of Eternity. The inspired writer of Ecclesiastes explains the struggle: "yet they cannot fathom what God has done from beginning to end." The prospect of Eternity leaves us bound in the dilemma of our own time structures. St. Augustine knew Eternity as a Christian, yet asked, "What then is time? If no one asks me, I know; if I wish to explain it to one that asks, I know not . . .."[19]

In studying Genesis, I, like others, have often been captivated by the events of our beginnings, missing the light that makes those events shimmer. I have fallen into American time traps of sequence and linear chronology, so much a part of my heritage but so inadequate for explaining Eternity. My American time concept sees a road upon which I am standing at the present looking back into the past and forward into the future. Event follows event. American progress, history and development are intricately woven into the fabric of my existence. Time is mathematical, full of numbers, dates and years adding up to the present. In Genesis, what happened when was more important to me than why it happened and who made it so.

Once, thinking my study had taken me beyond these trappings, I tried to explain the relationship of time and Eternity. A college class endured my feeble attempt to show the linkage on a two dimensional blackboard. Not surprisingly, I ended up with a very linear model straight out of my American heritage (See Figure 1A where a, b and c are special events linking time and Eternity). One perceptive student broke through the chalky dullness of the two-dimensional world of our blackboard by simply suggesting a timeline within a circle of Eternity.[20] (See Figure 1B on the next page).

If the circumference of the circle is seen as a mere convenience for the human eye, the circle of Eternity is seen as boundless light. Unlike my line, the circle suggests a content and a context, many dimensions and a multiplicity of directions. The difference is like seeing God bless our times with a thin beam of light from Eternity now and then or seeing him bless time by the powerful presence of an undying floodlight glow. Erich Sauer probably had a linear mind-set when he reverently said, "Eternity flows into time, even as time shall at last flow again into Eternity."[21] A new perspective encourages us to say, "Eternity glows throughout time, even as time shall at last glow throughout Eternity."

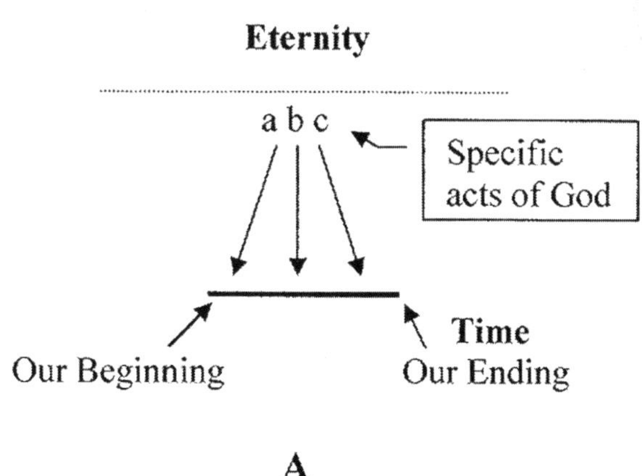


A

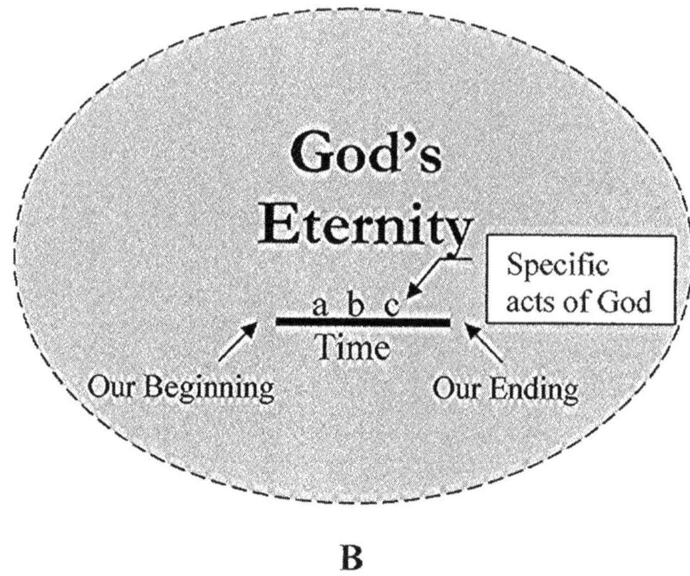


**B**

*Figure 1. Two Ways to See the Relationship of Time and Eternity.*

Why this attention to time and Eternity at the beginning of a book on culture and Kingdom? The answer is fundamental to our task. Culture is all about time and Kingdom is all about Eternity. That is why we must ask, What happened before time? What preceded Genesis? Before time, prior to Genesis, beyond the shadows of life lies the Kingdom empowering, inspiring, and enlightening us to the significance of our cultures, our times. Chapter Two looks more intently into this Kingdom, establishing its authority for living.

## FOR FURTHER STUDY AND DISCUSSION

1. *Which of the eight scriptures referring to "before the beginning" has the greatest impact upon you? Why?*
2. *Eternity as a great floodlight led to several applications in the text. Review these applications, then add others from your own reflection.*
3. *How would you define time? How has your understanding ever been in conflict with that of others?*
4. *Does reflection upon Eternity help put those conflicts into new perspective? What has changed?*

# Chapter 2

# GOD'S KINGDOM BEFORE THE BEGINNING

Like a powerful searchlight, the glow of Eternity brilliantly streams through every crack in time and shines behind every structure of our imaginations. Illuminating our darkness, enlightening our understanding, this glorious radiance before the beginning shining for us since our beginning is inhabited by God the King, his LIFE and his Kingdom. His brilliance and the Kingdom of glory are the standards against which we must measure our own little lights. King and Kingdom[22] are the content of Eternity.

God's LIFE exists unaffected by time barriers. "The Lord is King forever and ever," says the psalmist.[23]"He is the true God; the living God, the eternal King," declares the prophet.[24]"He is the King eternal, immortal, invisible, the only God, to whom there is honor and glory forever and ever," agrees the apostle.[25] Everything else, bound to time barriers, is measured against him.

In like manner, the Kingdom is eternal: "Your Kingdom is an everlasting Kingdom, and your dominion endures through all generations."[26] Strangely, God chose the humbled Nebuchadnezzar of Babylonia to convey this truth most graphically. In the course of describing a dream to Daniel, Nebuchadnezzar testified of God the King and his Kingdom, saying, "How great are his signs, how mighty his wonders! His Kingdom is an eternal Kingdom; his dominion endures from generation to generation."[27] The Most High God's Kingdom has no beginning, no end, and has always existed, just as he, the King has always existed.

## WHAT IS GOD'S KINDOM?

Because many Christian explanations of the Kingdom (*malkoth* in Hebrew, *basilea* in Greek) exist, one more definition may seem unnecessary. Study of the others, however, can lead us to recognize how these championed

**The Kingdom of God is far more than complex arguments of human experience in time and space.**

explanations usually become attached to cultural time and human centrality. Some define the Kingdom as a heavenly realm, a church domain, or a spiritual reality.[28] Others use moral, national and social definitions. Some make it a philosophical issue while still others relate the Kingdom to sectarian interests.

Consider another view:the Kingdom of God should neither be confused with nor confined to any of these approaches which ultimately elevate humanity. Although they may start with reference to God, their focus invariably shifts to the schemes and time frames of people.

For example, the Kingdom becomes related to a nation of people (the national), rewards for people (the heavenly), their institutions (the church), their religious nature (the spiritual), ethical lives (the Christian activists), the historical understanding of people (the philosophical), or the religious zeal of people (various sects). The concept of the Kingdom becomes tied up in complex arguments of human experience in time and space, especially that of the future. God's plan becomes adulterated with the plans of people, adjusted to meet their expectations. The Kingdom, however, is far more than any of these.

Common Christian consideration of the Kingdom is frequently related to the "millennium" or thousand-year reign of Christ mentioned in Revelation 20:1-6. Verse 6 says,

> Blessed and holy are those who have part in the first resurrection. The second death has no power over them, but they will be priests of God and of Christ and will reign with him for a thousand years.

The time and place of the thousand-year reign of Christ is important, but skewed focus has raised conflicting views dividing Christians over the centuries. One of my college professors used to contrast the pre-millennialists with the post-millennialists and end by saying, "I am a pro-millennialist." Interpretive methods and select Bible teachings have colored our understanding of the grand scope and comprehensiveness of God's Kingdom. We have become so immersed in our arguments and logic about the thousand-year reign that we fail to see the significance of the infinitely larger concept awaiting our discovery. Proponents of these millennial views are like the proverbial man who becomes so enamored with the trees that he does not see the forest, the millennium being a tree, the Kingdom the forest. Think of the millennium as a day in God's plan, but his Kingdom, beyond time-bound definitions, belonging to Eternity.[29] We need the larger vision.

God's rule or reign in time is another theme commonly found in Christian discussion of the Kingdom. Pre-millennialist George Ladd asserts his position, saying, "the Kingdom of God is the redemptive reign of God dynamically active to establish his rule among men. . . . This Kingdom, which will appear as an apocalyptic act at the end of the age, has already come into human history in the person and mission of Jesus."[30] Others argue that the Kingdom is not the reign or rule of God but his realm. Both arguments point to supportive Scripture.

God's reign is clearly stated, for example, in different scriptures: "He rules forever by his power, his eyes watch the nations, let not the rebellious rise up against him," - "The Lord has established his throne in heaven, and his Kingdom rules over all."[31]On the other hand, God's realm (location) is the subject of other verses " . . . live lives worthy of God, who calls you into his Kingdom and glory," - "The Lord will rescue me from every evil attack and will bring me safely to his heavenly Kingdom," - "For if you do these things, you will never fall, and you will receive a rich welcome into the eternal Kingdom of our Lord and Savior Jesus Christ."[32]

Certainly the Kingdom as God's reign and his realm needs to be included in any biblical understanding of the term, but another important aspect of the definition is often neglected or treated presumptuously. Taking us beyond cultural time frames, human centrality and the millennium, the Kingdom refers to God's eternal plan.

## GOD'S REASON BEHIND REIGN AND REALM

The Kingdom is God's reign, rule, and realm, but is also his *raison d'être*–his plan behind all reign and realm. This French word is defined as "reason of state" in a legal case, the basis of its argument.[33] Applied to this study, *raison d'état* is the reason behind the realm, God's grounds for his reign or rule. Time, space and events are important to reign and realm, but the Kingdom as *raison d'état* focuses our attention on the vision, the plan, the dream–and the Eternal LIFE behind it all. No mere abstract principle or ideal, the Kingdom issues from the very mind of God, his dynamic, deliberate, loving thought.[34]

**Taking us beyond cultural time frames, human centrality and the millennium, the Kingdom refers to God's eternal plan.**

Behind kingly power and position lies a LIFE-centered kingly plan and purpose. At the foundation of the kingly realm stands a LIFE-centered kingly *raison d'état.* Missionary scholar, E. Stanley Jones helps anchor the thought:"The Kingdom of God is the master-conception, the master-plan, the master-purpose, the master-will that gathers everything up into itself and gives it redemption, cohesion, purpose, goal."[35]

Rule, reign and realm are not excluded. Yet, repeated emphasis on these by theologians has led to divisive arguments of time, space and event. When does he rule? How does he reign? Where is his realm? The truth of God's action in time, space and event–initially, finally, and in all of history cannot be denied, but we need to get at the divine plan that activates these actions, the why. Reign and realm denote power, *raison d'être* indicates purpose and plan.

God's reason behind reign and realm rises from the wisdom Solomon quotes as saying, "The Lord possessed me at the beginning of his work, before his deeds of old; I was appointed from Eternity, from the beginning, before the world began."[36] This wisdom is not merely a collection of ideas floating above the course of human affairs, however; they are "creative deeds" of God's LIFE engaging human life.[37] As the psalmist and the prophet declare, "For he spoke, and it came to be; he commanded and it stood firm" – "But God made the earth by his power; he founded the world by his wisdom and stretched out the heavens by his understanding."[38] Isaiah adds his observation in 28:29 –" All this comes from the Lord Almighty, wonderful in counsel and magnificent in wisdom." Jesus Christ embodied that wisdom and was called the Word made flesh.[39] He perfectly portrayed the power, the purpose and the ultimate plan.

## A MYSTERY REVEALED

Does the Bible describe the Kingdom in terms of God's reason or plan? According to Howard Snyder whose definitive books on God's Kingdom have stirred the hearts of many, the book of Ephesians highlights this understanding.[40] Snyder explains that the Kingdom is God's *oikonomia*, his ultimate plan to unite all things, visible and invisible under the authority of Jesus Christ. Ephesians 1:9-10 says,

> **"The Kingdom is God's *oikonomia*, his ultimate plan to unite all things, visible and invisible under the authority of Jesus Christ."**
> *(Howard Snyder)*

> And he made known to us the mystery of his will according to his good pleasure, which he purposed in Christ, to be put into effect

> when the times will have reached their fulfillment - to bring all things in heaven and earth together under one head, even Christ.

Snyder says, "We learn more about the Kingdom when we view all of Scripture as the history of God's economy or plan to restore a fallen creation, bringing all God has made - woman, man, and their total environment - to the fulfillment of his purposes under his sovereign reign."[41]

The Kingdom as plan or purpose (*oikonomia*) was previously hidden from humankind's understanding, as the Apostle Paul says, "a mystery":

> We do, however, speak a message of wisdom among the mature, but not the wisdom of this age or of the rulers of this age, who are coming to nothing. No, we speak of God's secret wisdom, a wisdom that has been hidden and that God destined for our glory *before time began.* None of the rulers of this age understood it, for if they had, they would not have crucified the Lord of glory. However, as it is written:
>
> "No eye has seen,
> no ear has heard,
> no mind has conceived
> what God has prepared
> for those who love him"
>
> but God has revealed it to us by his Spirit. The Spirit searches all things, even the deep things of God. For who among men knows the thoughts of a man except the man's spirit within him? In the same way no one knows the thoughts of God except the Spirit of God.
>
> We have not received the spirit of the world but the Spirit who is from God that we may understand what God has freely given us. This is what we speak, not in words taught us by human wisdom but in words taught by the Spirit, expressing spiritual truths in spiritual words.[42]

Paul's calling and task was "to make plain to everyone the administration of this mystery."[43] He knew he was the one to whom the secrets had been given. Having glimpsed something of

**"No eye has seen,no ear has heard,
no mind has conceived
what God has prepared for
those who love him."**

that divine *raison d'être*, his life would never be the same. Definition, explanation and biblical reference to the Kingdom in this chapter prepare us to look at other important factors related to global issues. What is the content of the plan, for example? What are its central themes? How does it touch upon the diversity of human life in all the nations? Chapter Three continues our exploration and introduces us to the opening pages of the Bible in Genesis.

## FOR FURTHER STUDY AND DISCUSSION

1. *What is the Kingdom according to your church or individual study? What is the emphasis? Why?*
2. *Does the Kingdom seen as God's eternal plan contradict our previous view? Clarify it? Embrace it? How?*
3. *Using a concordance, discover other scriptures describing God's plan and purpose, his will and wisdom. Is it too far-fetched to say the Kingdom embraces all these? Why or why not?*
4. *How does the content of this chapter affect our consideration of global issues?*

# Part II

# LINKING GENESIS TO THE KINGDOM (GENESIS 1-2)

## Chapter 3

# OUR KINGDOM DESTINY IN GENESIS 1-2

Foundations are starting points, whether the activity involves the base upon which houses are built or blueprints for a new college. If a house is built in an east-west pattern, the foundation sets the direction. If a college practices certain policies, its foundation has established the principles. In the same way, two subjects, Eternity and the Kingdom, have now established the direction of our study. We need to lay the first block in place very carefully and start building upon this biblical base.

That first block, life, is central to both Kingdom and cultures. Genesis 1-2 forcefully bring this subject to our attention: first, the King's LIFE, then the life of his most favored creation.

## THE KING'S LIFE

"In the beginning God . . . "

What a mistake to read Genesis 1-2 and miss what they reveal about God's LIFE, God himself. In the popular defense of Creation versus evolution, Eternity and the Eternal One take a back seat to arguments about days and times. Most who do, focus upon the Creator seldom give attention to his LIFE and his Kingship. Why is that?

**What a mistake to read Genesis 1-2 and miss what they reveal about God himself.**

Some say God reveals himself as King much later in the biblical record and the linkage is not appropriate here. However, that later revelation is related to this earliest of records. "King" and "Kingdom" terminology is not dependent on human cultural experience of a later time for its legitimacy and significance to the Bible. Instead, these terms when used later point back to eternal absolutes. The cultural patterns of which they speak dimly reflect a condition that existed in the beginning.

Genesis 1-2 portrays the LIFE of God the King implicit in the sovereignty of his Kingdom. Out of his Eternity, God the King reveals himself in the truly stupendous act of "the beginning of time." Genesis marks the commencement of a kingly revelation which is nothing less than the eternal God helping us to know him–in time.[44] In Chapter One, God is referred to thirty-two times as *Elohim*. This plural form of the name points to the King as Father, Son and Holy Spirit. Psalm 33:6 clarifies, "By the word of the Lord were the heavens made, their starry hosts by the breath of His mouth." Associate the word with the Son, the Lord with the Father, and the breath with the Spirit. God is the eternal, all-encompassing King of Genesis1.

**God is the Creator-King of Genesis 1, the Covenant-King of Genesis 2. His royal life is the ultimate subject of both chapters.**

While Genesis 1 deals with the making of things and God is *Elohim*, Genesis 2 deals with the making of humankind, and God is called *Jehovah*. Chapter One shows him as the Creator-King; in Chapter Two he is the Covenant-King. The name *"Jehovah"* always identifies God in covenant relationship with humanity.[45]The nature of this covenant is seen in his very LIFE: God is love. As the Father, he loves and is the covenant-maker, as the Son he is loved and is the covenant respondent, and as the Holy Spirit he is love, the covenant promise itself–a perfect trinity in love.[46] Covenant love shows God in his fullness, the all-encompassing King of Genesis 2.

Whether as the Creator-King of Genesis 1, or the Covenant-King of Genesis 2, God's royal LIFE is the real subject of these introductory chapters of the Bible. Kingly purposes inspire the Creator. Powerful words and majestic action testify to the profoundness of a previous plan. He spoke and the world exploded into life according to that plan. Then he made humankind.

## MADE IN HIS IMAGE

Royal LIFE, kingly purposes, powerful words, majestic action–all these come to a focus with the creation of people. Consecrated life is the intent of our creation.

> So God created man in his own image, in the image of God he created him; male and female he created them.

What does it mean to be made in God's image? What does this have to do with life? How does it relate to God's LIFE?

The intent of Genesis 1:27 baffles Christians. Some explanations soar above the common views. I like Henri Blocher's observation that the image exists only because the Image Maker exists.[47] *Outside of God, human existence has no meaning.* "An image is only an image," he says, "*It exists only by derivation.* It is not the original, nor is it anything without the original". Because we are copies, not the original, our status is not only limited but also something of a mystery.

**In all God's creation, humans alone are appointed to bear the Creator's life, to be his only image-bearer.**

Another thought-provoking account comes from a study of the Greek word, *poema*, from which our English words "poem" and "poetry" derive.[48] In Romans 1:20, this Greek word refers to "things made." They are God's poetry, created to reveal himself <u>to</u> people. In Ephesians 2:10 the same word refers to the saved as God's "workmanship." Humanity, too, can be God's poetry. Unlike "things made," however, God reveals himself <u>through</u> people who will be his workmanship.

If we continue to explore the record, we must ask, Why are we made in God's image? While drawn to soaring views, I believe an important factor is often overlooked. That factor is God's own LIFE.

In all God's creation, humans alone are appointed to bear the Creator's LIFE, to be his only image-bearers–here is the heart of God's eternal plan for humanity. Behind the creation of humanity lies Kingdom purposes. God's existence would establish their direction, his nature would define their destiny. Most importantly, however, his own LIFE in them would make it all possible. Genesis 1-2 reveals not only God in his majesty but humanity in its destiny. Even angels and the rest of creation watch in wonder.[49]

**Our being made in God's image can best be understood by looking "<u>backward</u>" to Kingdom explanations of God's life, his intent and activity.**

LIFE-bearing life–this is the essence of "the image", a message that soars for me while others flop around on the ground, wingless. The difference is created by a growing Kingdom consciousness applied to Genesis 1-2. Many accounts do not take flight because they lack a passionate under-standing of God's Kingdom intentions for humanity. Our being made in God's image can best be understood not by looking forward from Genesis 1:27 to qualities of human life and to history, but by looking "backward" to Kingdom explanations of God's LIFE, his intent and activity. We must measure this act of God by the standards of Eternity, not of time. Unfortunately, many explanations begin with human life and temporal time. I will explain.

## KNOWING OUR DESTINY

Many explanations of the image assume that Adam and Eve were created as cultural beings and that some special quality of human life within those cultural conditions explains our being made in the Creator's image. In Chapter Five I will explain that this cultural precondition is erroneous. Here I will simply show how the assumption leads to poor interpretation.

Some writers describe the image in terms of freedom understood in time. Instead of beginning with an eternal perspective on freedom, they begin by admiring human ability to think and act freely in diverse cultural circumstances. The artist splashes paint on a canvas, the economist creates a new monetary pattern, the farmer creates a more efficient tool. Because we express freedom in our human experiences, we think this links us to God's freedom and is proof of being made in his image. Our destiny and the destiny of the nations is more than this, however.

Other scholars focus on love, saying our capacity to love evidenced in cultural settings is linked to God's love thus proving we are made in his image. Actually, human love can never reflect the divine. The uniqueness of God's LOVE is seen in the Old Testament word, *khesed* (a steadfast, covenant love, as well as mercy, loving-kindness and compassion). Translation consultant, Dr. Eugene Nida, reflects on the challenge of translating this into the languages of the world and concludes, "our best descriptions fall short of the full meaning . . .."[50] Human love and divine LOVE differ more than resemble each other. We don't discover the nature of the image by looking at human love in human time frames but by looking to the LOVE of God's LIFE and Eternity.

Still others link the image to human rationality. Since we assert our wills, express ourselves spiritually or rationally, are conscious of our humanness, have an understanding of immortality, or exhibit leadership, intelligence, power and relationships, we reflect God's image.[51] While rationality is expressed universally, the way we reason varies from culture to culture and we often make our cultural experience the standard, justifying our likeness to God.[52]

Many Americans, for example, think in *linear* fashion. Our conversations, arguments, lectures, sermons and books follow a similar pattern. We make a point, get right to it, and support it with a three-point outline and carefully crafted sub-points. Central to the occasion are our ideas. I work in Africa where people typically think *contextually*. That is, they observe an event and go all around the issue in socially correct behavior. Finally getting to the point, they will often support it by reference to *all* the contextual factors that may be relevant. Central to the occasion is the theme of relationship. I find the interchange fascinating.

I once went to a rural village in Zambia to "solve a problem" in a local church. This had unfortunately become part of my role as missionary. We Americans like to solve problems and use logical skills to do so. Once in the village, I greeted the man who had invited me. After some conversation, I asked, "Now, what is the problem?" The villager looked at me and smiled broadly.

"How is your wife?" he asked.

I must have been too hasty, so I stopped to answer his question. After some explanation, I asked, "What's the problem here at the church?"

Again, the Zambian looked at me and said, "How is your son?"

I was getting a little annoyed. He should know that we Americans are busy people and have many problems to solve. Why couldn't he get on with the situation? I answered him, however, and then got back to the problem. "That's why I have come," I told him.

He kept smiling and said, "How are the people at the church?"

This continued until finally we started discussing the problem–a leadership wrangle. That conversation, too, was very much around-the-bush. My American thinking patterns did not make me a good listener and more than once I thought, "Would you just get to the point." Linear rationality and contextual rationality–two ways of thinking. Which one is more in keeping with God's image?

**Does linear thought or contextual thought best represent God's image in us?**

When something like rationality is made the link to understanding our being made in God's image, we get into trouble by relating it to our own cultural standards that are not universal. As an American, I may think my linear form of rationality is the best and universal. Zambia taught me differently. Life in Africa required me to appreciate the complexities of contextual rationality in order to communicate there and the problem in that Zambian village did not get resolved until I submitted.

On the other hand, Africans may also believe their method of thinking is the best, and, should they apply it universally, decide it is next to godliness. Wrong. Other methods are predominant elsewhere in the world. Our particular mode of rationality is an unsuitable argument for our likeness to God.

The same kinds of complex differences are found in patterns of action, love, decisiveness and other elements of these cultures. Different expressions of universal features, say scholars, are evidence of our being made in God's image. Missing in discussions of freedom, love, human will and rationality is an eternal perspective sensitizing us to God's majestic LIFE and plan. If we begin by talking about possession of these qualities, we are time-bound.

**Our beginnings must be linked to Eternity, the Eternal King and God's Kingdom plan to share his LIFE with us.**

The starting point is important in our consideration of global issues. The foundation makes a difference. Our beginnings must be linked to Eternity, the Eternal King and God's Kingdom plan to share his very LIFE with us.

## KINGDOM LIVING

What happens when we allow God's existence to establish our direction, his nature to define our destiny? When the King's LIFE is preeminent, then human perspectives are subordinated to the eternal viewpoint.

This works very simply. The uniqueness of human rationality is still evident, of course. However, instead of elevating this capacity and pointing to cultural evidences linking divine origins to our own ways of thinking, we acknowledge God who wants us to bear his LIFE with his wisdom, knowledge and understanding. Being made in his image is to be consecrated, set apart for his LIFE.

**As God's image, we do not merely uphold culturally defined living. Instead we have *an ability to receive* a new Kingdom-defined LIFE into that living.**

In the same way, human freedom, though clearly evident, does not necessarily prove we are like God. After all, that freedom leads not only to courage, patriotism and sacrifice, but also to terror, immorality and selfishness. Instead, we have within us a place for a qualitatively different kind of freedom–one that corresponds in no way with human notions of freedom–God's freedom, Kingdom LIFE.

Love, will, spirituality, self-consciousness, the grasp of immortality, leadership, power and relationships–these frequently-held evidences of God's image in us actually point beyond something we have to something we don't have, which God wants to give us. These singular qualities do not assure us of being made in God's image. Their summation–call it life–only reminds us we were designed to attain another LIFE far beyond cultural limits.

Before our lives became dominated by competing human perspectives, the eternal viewpoint explained everything else, including our puzzling human nature. In being made in God's image, we do not merely uphold culturally defined living, but instead show *an ability to receive* Kingdom-defined LIFE into our lives.[53] Central to the Kingdom plan is God's intention to place his LIFE into our lives.

Our self-understanding begins with our understanding of God. Years of teaching African Christians led me to constantly reflect on my Western Christian identity. A popular contrast in these classes was Descartes' dictum for Western self-identity: *I think; therefore I am*, and John Mbiti's dictum for African self-identity: *We are; therefore I am.*[54] Then, one day, the Christian dictum leaped out of the pages of Scripture at me: *He is, therefore I am.*

How does Genesis 1-2 portray this destiny in the setting of a garden? Chapter Four views this scene from a growing Kingdom perspective.

## FOR FURTHER STUDY AND DISCUSSION

1. *The word, "Trinity" has come to be the key word for describing Father, Son and Holy Spirit. Compare this term with the names Elohim and Jehovah. Why are the names better than the abstract notion?*
2. *Self-identity is stretched in many directions these days. Background, experience, associations, work, achievements, aims–these do the pulling. How would you answer the question, "Who are you?"*
3. *What are the implications of Blocher's view of "the image"? Of its relationship to "God's workmanship?"*
4. *Have you usually understood "the image" in terms of one of the human qualities mentioned? Which one? Why?*
5. *Is there agreement in the world as to the meaning of human qualities like rationality and freedom? Illustrate some differences. How do they affect global issues?*
6. *Do you believe you were created to bear the Creator's very own LIFE? My Book, God's Dream: A Refreshing Look at the Gospel (Wine Press Publishing, 2011) elaborates on this in some depth.*

## Chapter 4

# GOD'S KINGDOM AND THE TREE OF *LIFE*

In Genesis 1-2, the Tree of LIFE growing in the middle of the garden is freely available to the still sinless Adam and Eve.[55] In Revelation 21-22, the Tree again appears, as part of the New Jerusalem. The leaves are for the healing of the nations.[56] What is the relationship of the Kingdom to the Tree of LIFE? Genesis 1-2 reveals answers to this question and aids our growing insight into the eternal Kingdom of God.

## GOD'S LIFE AS THE CENTRAL ISSUE

Fish move about in water, birds in air, animals on land. For each life, including human beings, God designed a unique environment. But the English language is limited with this word "life," sometimes hindering helpful distinctions. Whether we talk of the life of fish, birds, animals, insects, plants, germs or human beings, we use the same word. Our English word-crafters seemed to have lost their creativity at this crucial point. The most unfortunate reference is in regard to God, for in describing his own matchless character and nature, we use the same word.

The "life of" God is often merely a part of the religious terminology of Christians, something believed in as part of the doctrine and system of beliefs. That was the case for me for the first 24 years of my Christian life. Having learned about such things in Sunday School, church, and Bible college, I faithfully taught others what I learned, fostering a passive idea lacking power.

One day, in a country far removed from Sunday School, church and Bible college, while living and working with people of another culture and language, I learned my greatest lesson. More than a concept, a doctrine, part of a rational explanation of the world or even the best of religious thought, God's "life" stands as unique.

The culture and language of which I speak, the tradition of the Bemba people of Zambia, Africa, became part of my life between 1972 and 1979. The Bemba language has two words for life: *ubumi* and *umweo*, both having subtle nuances, the former referring to primal life, the latter to more general life. Bible translators used *ubumi* to translate eternal life (*ubumi bwa pe*) but also used *umweo* occasionally (*umweo wa muyayaya).* This use age of two words for life was a puzzle to me. Closer inspection, however, showed it to be closer to the original Greek than our English terminology. The Greek New Testament uses two primary words and reserves one solely for reference to eternal life–the word, *zoe.* Driven back to the Bible, I realized that God's LIFE is matchless and human language a poor vehicle for conveying the reality.

**Our King, bearing Kingdom LIFE, created human beings with whom to share that LIFE.**

The LIFE that takes center stage in Genesis 1-2 is this very LIFE of God (*zoe* in Greek and *ubumi* in Bemba), not that of Adam and Eve. Since English can't distinguish it from the life of a catfish, sparrow, or dog, I identify it by the capital letters LIFE and link it to the Kingdom. The King bears Kingdom LIFE. To designate its special quality, Jesus said, ". . . the Father has LIFE in himself."[57] One of his clearest references to his own deity lies in what follows: ". . . so he has granted the Son to have LIFE in himself." In fact, the Father-Son analogy is clarified here. They share the same LIFE.

Most remarkable of all is the glorious truth that the King, bearing Kingdom LIFE, created human beings with whom to share that LIFE. He designated himself as a gift for humankind from <u>before the beginning</u>. Describing the gift as eternal life (*zoe aionios*) in the New Testament, Paul makes clear the eternal intentions in Titus 1:1-3:

> Paul, a servant of God and an apostle of Jesus Christ for the faith of God's elect and the knowledge of the truth that leads to godliness–a faith and knowledge resting on the hope of eternal life, which God, who does not lie, promised *before the beginning of time*, and at his appointed season he brought his word to light through the preaching entrusted to me by the command of God our Savior (emphasis added).

Promised before the beginning of time, eternal LIFE was first intended for Adam and Eve in the Garden of Eden. They, like us, were created to share Kingdom LIFE with the LIFE-giver–to become Kingdom people having a Kingdom identity. Their means to that end stood, waiting for them, in the center of the Garden of Eden.

## THE TREE OF LIFE

How astonishing that in all the attention given to the Tree of the Knowledge of Good and Evil in the garden, the Tree of LIFE is often overlooked.[58] I have been surprised by the number of Christians who remember being taught about the former but not the latter. Yet, the Tree of LIFE flourished there, too, right in the center of the garden, available, to be freely fed upon *until sin changed the conditions*.

**Adam and Eve, like us, were created to share Kingdom LIFE with the LIFE-giver – to become Kingdom people having a Kingdom identity.**

> Now the Lord God had planted a garden in the east, in Eden; and there he put the man (and woman - Gen.1:27) he had formed. And the Lord God made all kinds of trees grow out of the ground–trees that were pleasing to the eye and good for food. In the middle of the garden were the tree of life and the tree of the knowledge of good and evil.[59]

What is the significance of the Tree of LIFE to Adam and Eve? What is the significance of LIFE? Just this: The first humans needed LIFE to be fully alive. DeVern F. Froneke states the case very clearly for Adam:

> It is important to understand that Adam as he came from the creative hand of God did not have divine life. Although created sinless, intelligent and happy, the first man and woman did not possess one tiny spark of the uncreated life of God . . ..[60]

Froneke describes Adam in four phases: "to be"–"become"–"share"–and "reign." True of Adam, these phases were also true of Eve. Beyond *being created*, Adam and Eve had to *become children*, sharing a common LIFE, in order to *participate* and *reign* in the Kingdom. Among other things, eating from the forbidden tree meant they failed in that additional calling and were separated from the LIFE of God–living souls, as Paul says of Adam,[61] but excluded from LIFE. Paul dwells on this extensively in 1 Corinthians 15 in his detailed contrast between the first Adam and the Last Adam. Becoming children, heirs and sovereigns–the very Kingdom intentions for humanity in God's image–was undermined and thwarted with Adam but was realized perfectly in Christ.

"The first man was not at first created in a condition of absolute perfection," says Erich Sauer.[62] Relating this to 1 Corinthians 15:45-46 as well, Sauer observes that Adam's sense laden body was "soulish" with qualities of intellect, emotion and will, but was not yet spiritual. Here, Sauer is shaking the Tree of LIFE. Only the LIFE of God can make humanity "spiritual," according to the Creator's will. Yet, this LIFE was missing in both Adam's and Eve's lives.

The breath of physical life (*bios*) from the Creator was wonderful. Yet, this gift was only the beginning of an eternal destiny in which they would be the recipient of the Creator's very own LIFE (*zoe*). They were neither perfect nor complete at creation – a radical departure from much prevalent theology. Though innocent and sinless, they were not yet as God intended them to be. Humanity was created good like all of creation, but the Creator was not yet done with them. Other creatures were finished but humankind was not.[63] Adam and Eve and all their progeny would remain God's premier workmanship.[64] To be complete, they needed the presence of God's LIFE. He created them to complete them.

**"The first man was not at first created in a condition of absolute perfection"** *(Erich Sauer).*

This leads to the well-known command of Genesis 2:16-17 -

> And the Lord God commanded the man, "You are free to eat from any tree in the garden; but you must not eat from the tree of the knowledge of good and evil, for when you eat of it you will surely die."

We often interpret this command with little consideration or understanding of its Kingdom context. Here, God is setting out to implement his master-plan through Adam and Eve. When seen as part of God's Kingdom intentions, the precept of the command is enlightened by the promise of the covenant relationship. The first words of promise then glow brightly: "You are free" (NIV) or "You may freely eat" (New Oxford Annotated Bible). Adam and Eve were invited to eat the fruit of all the other trees, including the Tree of LIFE.

**The precept of the command in Genesis 2:16-17 is enlightened by the promise of the covenant relationship.**

Common attention to the command of Genesis 3:16-17 draws interest to the Tree of the Knowledge of Good and Evil, emphasizing what Adam was not to have done. The negative blinds us to the positive, however. Seeing the Scripture within a Kingdom perspective draws attention to the Tree of LIFE which emphasizes what Adam was to have done.

What did God desire of Adam and Eve? Clearly, that they would take and eat from the Tree of LIFE, not by his command but by the volition of free choice. Placed in the middle of the garden, this tree surely attracted them. Named by God as the "Tree of LIFE," it surely aroused some curiosity in the original pair. Beyond attraction or curiosity, God intended that they would take from the Tree of LIFE–freely. In that taking would be the completion of physical life and the reception of eternal LIFE. They would move from mere human personality to Kingdom personality, from a created, human sameness to a Kingdom identity, from "living souls" to LIFE-bearing images of God. They were to recognize that God's LIFE was essential to complete human life. In that spontaneous taking would be fulfillment of God's dream for his human creation.[65]

**"It takes God to be a man"** *(Ian Thomas)*

Like Adam and Eve, we need God's LIFE to be fully alive today. As W. Ian Thomas has said, "It takes God to be a man."[66] John puts it simply in 1 John 5:12 - "He who has the Son has LIFE; he who does not have the Son of God does not have LIFE." The culmination of God's dream awaits our reception of his LIFE. How does this occur?

## WHEN GOD'S *LIFE* DWELLS IN HUMAN LIFE

Once we recognize the reality of God's gift, we can ask how to receive and live by his generosity and grace. LIFE is available; how can we experience such a gift? Where, besides just in our minds and systems of belief can we apply LIFE made real, palpable, energetic? How does this relate to the global issues of our concern? A brief diversion from Genesis clarifies the issue, preparing us to look more intently at the unfolding relationship of God's Kingdom and our cultures.

The human spirit is the focal point for all reflection on Kingdom LIFE in the human personality. The word "spirit" occurs about 750 times in the Bible. It is translated from the Hebrew, *ruach*, in the Old Testament and the Greek, *pneuma*, in the New. Either God's Spirit or human spirit is meant, with half the references being to human spirit.[67] Bible scholars argue about the position of the human spirit in human personality and the relationships of body, soul, spirit and heart. Hebrews 4:12 indicates, however, that whatever the scholarly assessment, *the human spirit is distinct from the soul* in a way understood fully only by God.

When the Bible refers to the human spirit, it usually does so in a context of intimate relationship to God. For example, when the Old Testament uses *ruach* to refer to either God or people, the dynamic relationship between both is intended.[68] When Jesus said, "God is Spirit and they that worship him must worship him in spirit and in truth,"[69] he continues the Old Testament portrayal of Divine Spirit and human spirit bound together in a unity of purpose.

**Created personality becomes Kingdom personality when the human spirit accepts LIFE.**

Most importantly, the human spirit was created to be the dwelling place of God–his royal residence in human personality. By God's design, the human spirit enables us to receive and to be motivated by the very LIFE of God Himself, to become Kingdom people with Kingdom identity. Perhaps this is the meaning of Proverbs 20:27, "The spirit of man is the candle of the Lord . . .". The words of Jesus now move us deeply when he says: "You are the light of the world."[70] The human spirit is like a lamp that cannot produce light by itself, but once touched by the LIFE intended to work in and through it, the human spirit reflects light in total contrast to the former darkness. The human spirit finds fulfillment in human personality only when accomplishing God's intended purpose–to be the receptacle of God's gift of LIFE.

Created personality becomes Kingdom personality when the human spirit accepts LIFE through the Holy Spirit's action upon that spirit.[71] Charles Wesley's inspiring hymn describes the impact:

> Long my spirit lay fast bound
> in sin and nature's night;
> thine eye diffused a quickening ray –
> I woke, the dungeon flamed with light;
> my chains fell off, my heart was free.
> I rose, went forth,
> and followed thee.[72]

Accepting this gift by hearing, believing and accepting the redemptive conditions of Jesus Christ, we become Kingdom people. Our life is blessed with his LIFE. Our human identity is linked to God's image not human expectations, and our destiny connects with his eternal plan.

Bound to the King in eternal covenant, we can demonstrate the Kingdom plan in our earthly activity. All of this relates to Christian impact on global issues.

## THROUGH *LIFE* COMES KNOWLEDGE

God's desire can be stated in a principle which stands at the heart of the Kingdom perspective set forth in this book: through LIFE humankind shall have KNOWLEDGE.[73] In other words, God comes first; knowledge is related to him. His desire contrasts to an opposing principle to be studied in the chapters that follow, a principle linked to the Tree of Knowledge, which states, "through knowledge humankind shall have life." Note the exchange of LIFE for knowledge, of KNOWLEDGE for life in these conflicting desires. As it works out in life, knowledge first yields disastrous consequences. When God's principle is implemented, LIFE engages life and KNOWLEDGE propels knowledge. How is this so?

From before the beginning, the Kingdom plan sees God's own LIFE as the basis of KNOWLEDGE emerging from God's wisdom. LIFE, the very expression of holiness, would be the model as well as the basis for human holiness. Intimate personal sharing of LIFE would be the prerequisite for any sharing of KNOWLEDGE. The principle still held thousands of years later when Jesus would say, "Now this is eternal life: that they may know you, the only true God, and Jesus Christ, whom you have sent."[74] We can know him because he is there to be known.

LIFE must come first if the Kingdom of God is to prevail. LIFE animates life. LOVE gives direction to love, JOY to joy, FREEDOM to freedom, HOPE to hope. Life animated by LIFE is exaltation, all else is mere existence. We rejoice in his constant presence, marvel at his abiding strength, see his way and know our direction by reliance on the revelation of his LIFE. Never alone, life animated by LIFE is a constant fellowship with the source of both.

KNOWLEDGE following upon LIFE exists in a covenantal relationship and depends on God's revelation. We KNOW what God reveals. With such KNOWLEDGE we see good and evil in the world by the measuring rod of God's LIFE instead of our own. We are blessed by his appraisal of right and wrong, not our own experience.

**We begin to see good and evil in the world by the measuring rod of God's LIFE instead of our own.**

In America we are torn by an ethic that upholds tolerance for differences yet seeks the unity of our nation.[75] When do tolerance and unity become evil? By what standard do we measure them as good? Answering these questions torments our souls. Other nations confront equally complex contradictions. The citizens of some want security provided by strong police and military forces only to find those same forces entrenched against them. Others want development but are subject to available resources as limited as they are. Confined to life only, we can expect the conflict of lives because answers will vary as much as the dynamics around us. When LIFE is added to our understanding of life, however, knowledge is blessed with KNOWLEDGE. Reason encounters revelation.

God's solution to these contradictions is simple: through LIFE humanity shall acquire KNOWLEDGE. Shared, covenantal relationship was always his intent for the epitome of his creation. Tolerance, unity, security, power, development and the stewardship of resources must be defined by the Kingdom. The King defines them, his LIFE provides their measure. God intends for his KNOWLEDGE to pervade all of life–all that we today call economics, technology, social systems, communications, language, politics and even religion. The provision, however, is always on the basis of his admonition to "Seek first the Kingdom . . .".

Genesis 1-2 describes Kingdom conditions, not a cultural environment as is commonly assumed. In these chapters we have seen that creation 1) shows that humankind made in God's image has Kingdom explanations, and 2) God's gift of LIFE is central to the Kingdom perspective of this book, even the key to a principle or aim found first in Genesis 2: through LIFE humankind shall have KNOWLEDGE.

Immediately evident is the fact that Adam and Eve, and thus humankind, missed the blessings God intended for them. How did that happen? Why did it occur? What were its consequences? Are the blessings still available? These questions propel us to Chapter Five.

## FOR FURTHER STUDY AND DISCUSSION

1. *Reflect upon your own study of Genesis 1-2. Which tree has been emphasized most for you? What do you think are the consequences upon your life?*
2. *List the author's statements about Adam and Eve. Which ones represent those commonly known to you? Which ones strike you as new?*
3. *Do you believe that God's LIFE is essential to complete human life?*
4. *Consider the application of the principle, through LIFE humankind shall have KNOWLEDGE. How would economics be different? Technology? The social system? Communications? Language? Politics? Religion? (The author has written two other books that address these issues: Kingdom Faith: Breaking Through Religious Boundaries and The Kingdom Mandate: Foundations for Transformational Stewardship.*

## Part III

# LINKING OUR CULTURES TO GENESIS

Chapter 5

# OUR CULTURES AND THE TREE OF KNOWLEDGE

If the foundation of a building is laid out in an east-west direction, that determines how the building will lie. Sometimes, later plans dictate additions to be attached here and there. In fact, too many extensions may change the building's appearance altogether. No longer having a basic east-west orientation, the old foundation loses significance.

This is the case with God's Kingdom foundation for humanity. Capricious human additions have skewed God's original design.

What are the additions? Who added them? How did they skew the Kingdom foundation of God's plan? Genesis Chapter Three provides a basis for answering these questions. Our cultures are the additions humanity in all its diversity has made and the skewing is a never-ending interference with God's intentions.

To recognize the significance of Genesis Three, I must overcome a common assumption among Christians. The presupposition that spoils our view is that God created Adam and Eve and set them in a cultural environment of his making. The Garden, language, relationships, food, instructions, religious observance–all these are presumed to be evidence of the first culture. I challenge this assumption. Genesis Three, not Genesis One, is the place to look for the first cultural patterns.

From Genesis Three we can glimpse the basic nature of all cultures. The empowering principle common to every culture, whether of the ancient Egyptians or of modern Europeans, is evident in this chapter. Here, we find the most hellish of Satan's activity and the most hapless of humanity's. Here, we are helped to understand human personalities, the stranglehold of world view assumptions, and the nature of divinely imposed limitations to humankind's development. Genesis Three introduces us to cultures–human patterns of living in different environments.

**From Genesis Three we can glimpse the basic nature of all cultures.**

## OUR CULTURES AND HUMAN KNOWLEDGE

This definition of cultures is only one among many. At least 200 different definitions of the subject existed as of 1963.[76] Evolution, history, archeology, personality, religion, social organization, symbolism, communication, economics, politics and ecology have influenced these definitions at different times since the mid-1800s. Probably another 200 definitions have been produced in the last 50 years.

**Definition of cultures as used in this book–human patterns of living in different environments.**

Human patterns of living in different environments–to this simple definition we must now add the ingredient of knowledge. James P. Spradley and David W. McCurdy, for example, define cultures as "the acquired knowledge that people use to interpret experience and to generate behavior."[77] Cultural patterns are learned and exist from childhood at different levels of awareness.[78] Christian anthropologist, Marvin Mayers and sociologist Stephen Grunlan define a culture as "the learned and shared attitudes, values, and behaviors of a society."[79]–patterns of living.

A given culture is a pattern of living learned in a specific environment. Consider a girl born among the Bemba people of Zambia. She learns acceptable attitudes, information and behavior in the earliest stages of growth. For example, a spirit of communal involvement is an acceptable attitude. Her mother-tongue becomes the medium for songs and riddles that teach her the necessary information. In behavior she learns to be submissive to those older than she. As she matures, she uses these patterns to relate to life around her and to express her own distinct self in the midst of these patterns. The child acquires a culture, a system of knowledge which experts describe as a universal pattern in terms of religion, education, communication, economic systems, technology, society, the politics of leadership and ecology. When she raises food to her mouth, she expresses a cultural pattern unique to her people. When she buys a school bag, she does the same.

Out of all the possibilities for patterns of life, a group like the Bemba agree upon a limited number of patterns. In the young girl's traditional culture, religion centers around belief in one supreme God whom they call *Lesa*. Education focuses upon the training of children and youth by relatives. Men teach young boys as they tell of exploits and repeat old stories while sitting in the rest shelters or around evening fires. Grandmothers and aunts teach Bemba girls using an elaborate collection of symbolic artifacts. Communication is expressed in rhythmic, musical ways with words flowing easily into riddles, proverbs and songs. Agricultural activities such as hoeing, planting and harvesting by hand occupy much of their time. Societal and political relationships may be characterized by gestures of politeness, respect, and clearly defined authority. Land and rivers become the single most important symbol in the ecological environment as streams provide natural boundaries between families and clans.

**Out of all the possibilities for patterns of life, a group like the Bemba agree upon a limited number of patterns.**

The young girl from toddlerhood up learns the patterns of her culture quickly and efficiently. Outside her culture, however, she would discover that different designs apply. Were she to visit India, for example, she would learn that many gods are recognized and a whole new set of symbols must be considered. Instead of family members, educational institutions provide symbols, strange sounds and a completely different rhythm that the young girl would need to learn. Indian economy, trade and commercial activity requires different kinds of patterns to be learned. Politeness, respect and authority are there, but the designs all differ. Land is seen in terms of different values.

Though acquired knowledge is fundamental to the life of people in a given culture, that knowledge is arbitrary, say Spradley and McCurdy. Relevance to one group of people does not always resonate for another group even within their own culture.

The point here is that knowledge is central to anthropological discussion of cultures. Is it also central to a biblical understanding?

## THE BIBLE AND HUMAN KNOWLEDGE

The concept of cultures as learned patterns of living is also central to the Bible. Genesis Three provides this understanding, the key verse being Genesis 2:16-17–

> You are free to eat from any tree in the garden; but you must not eat from the tree of the knowledge of good and evil, for when you eat of it you will surely die.

The Tree of the Knowledge of Good and Evil in the Bible's Genesis account represents my seminal reason for defining cultures in terms of knowledge.

We know the rest of the story in Genesis. Adam and Eve disobeyed God, ignored the Tree of LIFE and ate from the forbidden tree. We often miss the implications. We recognize the beginnings of sin, but *fail to see in these events the beginnings of our cultures*. The rest of the story includes this beginning.

**The Tree of Knowledge in the Bible's Genesis account represents my seminal reason for defining cultures in terms of knowledge.**

What are cultures but a society's rationale of good and evil, right and wrong established and imprinted in patterns of living? Hard work is good and thievery is evil. Respect for others is right and indifference is wrong. What better explanation of the thousands of cultures that have given order to human endeavor in all the corners of the world and in all the generations of humankind descending from Adam? Each is a pattern for a group's estimate of right and wrong. Commonalities, symbolic expression, language, loyalties, development, expansion, migration, change, misunderstandings, divisions, segmentation, competition, even wars–do they not evolve out of human perception of what we regard as good and evil?

When did knowledge become part of the concept? In Genesis Three with Adam and Eve's sin. At the heart of this beginning is the denial of God's foundational principle for humanity that through LIFE we shall KNOW. God's postulate is skewed, a new principle is asserted. Wisdom from God is replaced by the human pursuit of knowledge.

## CAN KNOWLEDGE LEAD TO LIFE?

Adam and Eve's response to the covenant command of Genesis 2:16-17 provides the grounds upon which to understand the development of our cultures in all generations. Ignoring the Tree of LIFE from which they could have eaten freely in their innocent state, the first humans chose the Tree of Knowledge. Rather than seeking LIFE that would result in KNOWLEDGE, they sought knowledge, thinking thereby to gain life. Life replaced LIFE; knowledge replaced KNOWLEDGE. This deplorable response set in place a struggle for God's creation that has endured ever since. Adam and Eve initiated a wrongly focused principle at the very heart of all cultures:through knowledge we shall have life.

**In glaring contrast to God's Kingdom plan, the cultural principle claims that knowledge leads to life.**

In glaring contrast to God's Kingdom plan, the cultural principle was not only a choice for the first man and woman of Genesis, but every generation since has faced this fundamental issue lying at the heart of every culture. People in their cultures, lacking all knowledge of the Kingdom, assume that if only sufficient things are known–in the social realm, the political, the economic, the technological, the religious, the communicational–then they will live successfully

All this in spite of the fact that God had warned, "when (or, in the day that) you eat of the tree of the knowledge of good and evil you will surely die." How could Adam and Eve have been so misled? Let us look more deeply into the events of Genesis Three.

## SATAN AND OUR HUMAN-CENTERED KNOWLEDGE

The first man and woman were seduced to an acquisition of knowledge indifferent to God and from a source outside of God. That seducer and the source was Satan. Readers may protest this connection between cultures and Satan, which seems to disparage and malign cultures, but a fresh consideration of Satan shows this is not necessarily so.

The most common stereotype of Satan portrays him as a red-suited devil with pointed ears, tail, horns and hoofs, seen as one reveling in everything that is ugly, cruel, vicious and unclean. Indeed, the Bible calls him the destroying angel, great dragon, deceiver of the whole world, and accuser of the brethren.[80]

Though we usually associate Satan with hell, he actually wants to be the god of heaven. He did not and does not want to be a fiend but a friend, not unlike God but like him. "He is the inspirer and instigator of the very highest standards of the God-less, self-made world of mankind."[81] A subtle seducer.

Satan wants a world immersed in the supernatural; he wants a "good" religious world. As long ago as 1919, seminarian L.S. Chafer said Satan "is the very embodiment of the highest ideals that the unregenerate world has received, for he is the inspirer of all those ideals."[82] Chafer went on to make clear that Satan wants to make this time of his opportunity as good as possible–but totally without God:

**Satan wants a world immersed in the supernatural; he wants a "good" religious world.**

> Satan's ideal of this age is then, an improved social order, a moral and cultured people . . .. The Satanic message for this age will be reformation and self-development, while the message of God is regeneration by the power of the Spirit.[83]

As we navigate the twenty-first century, Satan's hidden plans still hold true today.

When it comes to cultures, Satan may be considered an expert on our cultural ways.[84] He makes good use of human-centered cultural plans and patterns. Look at Genesis 3:1 for a correct perspective on this enemy of God.

> Now the serpent was more crafty than any of the wild animals the Lord God had made. He said to the woman, "Did God really say, 'You must not eat from any tree in the garden?"

**Satan makes good use of human-centered cultural plans and patterns.**

Crafty. Here we see Satan skillfully plying his trade. The garden was a strategic place for implementing his alternative design for the universe because in Eden God brought his Kingdom into the realm of time and space. The eternal plan, the very expression of God's nature, the introduction of LIFE, a covenant that leaves Satan out forever–all are found in the garden, a challenge for Satan's "best." Having rebelled against the Kingdom plan in heaven, he had to oppose it on earth. After all, it was on earth, not in heaven, that the plan would be initiated. In humanity, not in angels like himself, would LIFE join with life according to God's plan.

Perhaps we will never fathom the conflict in its entirety. W. Ian Thomas gives us a glimpse in The Mystery of Godliness, where he observed that Satan's attitude here was arrogant self-sufficiency.[85] For Satan, the Creator was not necessary to the creation, nor was the creation responsible to the Creator. His strategy, then, was simply to introduce this same attitude into the new earthly situation, convincing Adam and Eve that they could "be God-like without being God-conscious,"[86] that in themselves they were adequate for knowing good without any recourse to God; that they could be righteous in their own eyes whether or not they had God's LIFE within. Dismissing God, Satan implied they could still have everything. Dominion over all creation would be theirs without being subject to the demands of the Creator. They could enjoy the liberty of their intellects, emotions, and wills, without having to rely on the LIFE of God. The hidden agenda, of course, involved the trading of dependence on God for independence from God. Who needed the Tree of LIFE when they had the Tree of Knowledge?

Satan's activity is centered upon a clever entrapment of humanity. Never able to create cultures the way people do, he works to ensnare us in our own creations, employing our temptation to be "self-made" people worshipping ourselves, whether as rugged individuals in America or as similarly self-invented groups of people in other parts of the world.

Cultures are not evil, as association with Satan might lead a reader to believe. The mortal danger is that cultures are good–but in a way that excludes God or places him in a convenient place of the culture's making. Cultures are another good, the greatest threat to humanity's recognition of and desire for the Kingdom. They provide an alternate plan, partnership and principle–goodness without godliness; as Thomas says, our "good" to the exclusion of God's. Dr. Sherwood Lingenfelter, Christian anthropologist graphically portrays this truth in his book, Transforming Culture: A Challenge for Christian Mission. After holding to a positive and neutral view of cultures for many years, he gradually accepted their negative side and now boldly calls them, "prisons of disobedience."[87] In a workshop once held in Kenya, he clarified: "The prison is not a murky dungeon, however; it is a palace surrounding us with multiple comforts."[88]

**Cultures are not evil, as association with Satan might lead a reader to believe. The mortal danger is that cultures are good – but in a way that excludes God.**

Satan knows the subtlety of cultural entrapment for humanity and he applies his own brand of anthropology for the continuing expansion of cultures minus the King and his Kingdom. The pride of knowledge fits nicely into his own kind of development. His strategy leads to a disguised bondage of human personalities, the subject of Chapter Six.

## FOR FURTHER STUDY AND DISCUSSION

1. *Can you identify a culture central to your life whereby people share patterns of living? What do you call it? How does it differ from others you know?*
2. *How is shared knowledge central to this culture you describe?*
3. *Can you describe this culture in terms of what its people think is good and evil, right and wrong?*
4. *Consider the contrasting principles: 1) Through LIFE we shall KNOW and 2) Through knowledge we shall live. Do they clarify the tension between God's Kingdom and our cultures for you? Why or why not?*
5. *Which of the following statements is true according to the text: 1) Satan creates culture, or 2) Humans create culture? Why is the difference important?*
6. *How can Christians see the good in cultures and still recognize their dangers? Discuss this with others.*
7. *How does this chapter's content impact our discussion of global issues?*

## Chapter 6

# THE DOMINANCE OF CULTURAL PERSONALITIES

"Men are from Mars, women are from Venus," says John Gray in his 1992 best-seller.[89] Men and women think, respond, feel, react, love and appreciate differently. "They almost seem to be from different planets," he observes as he embarks on describing ways of improving relationships. Discussing Gray's idea with colleagues in Africa, both American and African, we agreed that the author should qualify his description as "American." African men and women are not necessarily from Mars or Venus, maybe from Jupiter and Mercury. Men from Mars and Jupiter sometimes have difficulty in communicating with each other, as do women from Venus and Mercury. Resemblances abound, of course, but differences exist and need our attention.

For example, we all speak and act from an assumed center of our lives, affections, and values. We express this commonality in different ways, however, and in that very expression there exists a subtle difference of self-identity. For Americans, the heart is central. We love, grieve, become angry and rejoice with the heart. To hear Paul say, "clothe yourselves with bowels of mercy" in Colossians 3:12 (KJV) seems vulgar and meaningless. We prefer a reference to the heart. Other body organs may take center stage for other nationalities: the stomach for the Conob of Guatamala, the throat for the Bemba of Zambia, the liver for the Karre people of West Africa and even the kidneys and gall bladder.[90] Imagine an American courting his girl, "I love you with all my gall bladder." In other languages and cultures, this organ is the most central, the heart superficial.

Explanations for both the resemblances and differences of cultures exist in Genesis 1-3 and are grounded in a deeper lesson. God's intention for Kingdom personalities dominates the first two chapters of Genesis; cultures and cultural personalities expose their foundations in Genesis Three. The two contrasting plans for human development compete. One plan proclaims the adequacy of life and knowledge without God, providing a prison of disobedience disguised as a palace. The other announces the gift of LIFE and KNOWLEDGE opening gates and grates, unlocking windows, removing walls, presenting a grand freedom.

## SELF-IDENTITY IN HUMAN CULTURES

Cultural personalities depending on human images and models contrast with the Kingdom personality based on God's image and described in Chapter Four. The King is central to Kingdom identity and his plan energizes all activity on earth. Kingdom stewardship motivates Kingdom people and covenant relationship binds the human personality to God and to others. God's LIFE in human life is essential to satisfaction and the condition upon which all other fulfillment ultimately depends. LIFE is the source of KNOWLEDGE dependent on God's perspective and his revelation.

**God's intention for Kingdom personalities dominate the first two chapters of Genesis; cultures and cultural personalities expose their foundations in Genesis Three.**

Cultural personalities came into clear focus when the first man and woman chose to eat from the forbidden tree. The identities they favored still dominate our lives today.

> When the woman saw that the fruit of the tree was good for food and pleasing to the eye, and also desirable for gaining wisdom, she took some and ate it. She also gave some to her husband, who was with her, and he ate it.[91]

Now they were no longer the innocents they had been before their rebellion. When they swallowed the fruit they swallowed a new dimension of self-directing knowledge.

This knowledge gained by earth's first man and woman was not simply intellectual ability. Rather, the Hebrew word for knowledge, *da'ath*, in Genesis 2 and 3 comes from *yada*–intimate, personal knowledge. "To ascertain by seeing," says Strong's Concise Dictionary of the Words in the Hebrew Bible.[92]The knowledge offered by the forbidden tree was a moral, experiential, philosophical knowledge turned inward to the self, not outwardly to God. Connoting cunning and wit, this was knowledge discovered on one's own–explored, tasted and tried. That would not be so bad except for the fact that

**Cultural personality seeks the fulfillment of life on the human level alone and the pursuit of knowledge is the way to that life.**

it is the knowledge of both good <u>and</u> evil on this basis. Before this, Adam and Eve could perceive evil based on God's righteous judgment revealed to them. Henceforth they would know evil, as well as good, by their own exploration. This is the nature of personality dominated by cultures where our aim becomes the pursuit of knowledge for life.

No abstract notion is portrayed here; you and I can relate to this experience every day of our lives. As children we took warnings to the limit, touching what was not to be touched for example–hot, delicate, personal, that above us, below us. *Yada.* As youth, we became more secretive and subtle, still exploring the limits of right and wrong–our own way. *Yada.* As adults, the unending search goes on at work, play, alone, with others. *Yada.* Like Adam and Eve, we reverse the "God has said" to "Has God said?" and challenge the limits.

**The knowledge offered by the forbidden tree was a moral, experiential, philosophical knowledge turned inward to the self, not outwardly to God.**

Cultural personalities rise out of the human pursuit of knowledge begun by Adam and Eve *where identity relies on human estimates of good and evil.* No longer reflecting God as central, these personalities depend on identities created and maintained by people in social, racial, religious and economic realms. Diverse cultural plans *not* of God's making energize their activity. These personalities bear fruit, subdue the earth and rule over other creatures for the approval of other humans first, not God. Human socialization, not stewardship, provides the criteria for "good" living. People are "good" if they live by the rules of the society. Consensus among people, not covenant relationship with God and others, binds human personality to others first and to God only as an afterthought. American consensus results in American-type personalities; African consensus results in African-type personalities. God's LIFE, absent from human life in the extreme expression of these personalities, is not recognized as essential for vitality, even though lip service is paid to God in pious gestures. Instead, cultural personality seeks the fulfillment of life on the human level alone and the pursuit of knowledge the way to that life. Table 1 shows the contrasts.

Table 1. Contrasting Identities

| Kingdom Personality | Cultural Personalities |
|---|---|
| Based on God's image | Based on human images |
| The King is central | People are central |
| God determines good/evil | People determine good/evil |
| God's approval sought | Human approval sought |
| Covenant relationships | Consensual relationships |
| LIFE leads to KNOWLEDGE | Knowledge leads to life |
| LIFE is essential | LIFE is usually not recognized |

Let's consider the cultural personality of the African girl described earlier. From the time of birth her identity with an extended family, clan and ethnic group is intensified day-by-day. "A frog does not leave its water-hole," say her teachers, and a child remains true to family and tribe. She learns her place in economic and technological activities that foster the well-being of her society. "The bird that sings well is not always the best nest builder," declares another proverb, meaning, "A good talker is not necessarily a good worker." The consensus of beliefs, values and norms that characterize her people are carefully handed down to her. She is reminded of her need to learn these from others: "The armpit is not above the shoulder." Knowledge is passed on with the assumption that it will result in further life for her and the group. Her brother learns similar identity with male norms and values emphasized. Although God (*Lesa*) has a place in her identity, activity, religious understanding, knowledge and life, his place is defined and determined by the people around the young girl.

**A frog does not leave its waterhole.**
**The armpit is not above the shoulder.**
*(African Proverbs)*

What is true of the young African child is true of every child, girl or boy, in every society. Educators, psychologists, psychoanalysts, and psychiatrists specialize in the development of cultural personalities. Universities, foundations and businesses thrive on the subject. Libraries and bookstores abound with books about cultural personalities. These specialists and places operate without recognizing that cultural personalities are only part of the reality. Ephesians 4:17-18 describes this situation:

> So I tell you this, and insist on it in the Lord, that you must no longer live as the Gentiles do, in the futility of their thinking. They are darkened in their understanding and separated from the LIFE of God because of the ignorance that is in them due to the hardening of their hearts.

Or, is it the hardening of stomachs, livers and gall bladders? Whatever, cultural personalities are about life minus LIFE or, at best, life dominating LIFE. To understand them we need a biblical knowledge of Kingdom personality.

Relating the events of Genesis Three to ourselves and seeing that the woman sought something good to eat, pleasing to the eye, and useful for wisdom, we ask, "What aspect of human personality is drawn to knowledge so central to cultures? Is it our heart, intellect, will–maybe the gall bladder? Do these events help us understand?"

**Cultural personalities are about life minus LIFE or, at best, life dominating LIFE.**

## THE APPEAL OF KNOWLEDGE

The Bible portrays the soul as the aspect of personality related to knowledge. Just as humans were created with a spirit capacity for God's LIFE, so they were also created with a soulish capacity for God's KNOWLEDGE. Divorced from God's plan, however, both spirit and soul become twisted caricatures of God's intentions.

Ruth Paxson's classic book, Life on the Highest Plane, presents the soul as center of our self-consciousness, the spirit as center of our God-consciousness, and the body as center of our world-consciousness. She sees the soul as God's intended mediator uniting spirit and body, a channel through which they interact with each other. The soul stands "midway between two worlds," she says.[93] Through the body the soul is linked to the visible and earthly; through the spirit it is linked with the unseen and heavenly.

Sin in the Garden of Eden changed the nature of the soul's position in human personality. A new centrality no longer focused upon the necessity of LIFE in the spirit mediating to the body. Now attention was upon

**Sin in the Garden of Eden changed the nature of the soul's position in human personality.**

the mere niceties of life which had their origin in the soul: intellect, emotion and will. Self-consciousness took precedence over God-consciousness. Knowledge became more important than KNOWLEDGE.

"In rebelling against God," says Watchman Nee, "Adam and Eve developed their souls to the extent of displacing their spirits and plunging themselves into darkness."[94]They became over-developed in their souls. No longer would they simply be living souls, but from henceforth would "live by the soul," Nee clarifies in another volume.[95] They would live so as to please their own desire for knowledge, emotional expression and volitional determination. They would satisfy their souls and spirits in their way rather than in God's way, abusing the freedom of choice with which they were created.

The consequences of such self-satisfaction are described in a parable circulating in Kenya. A grocer had a good business in a small community even though a competitor was likewise thriving across the road. God came to the grocer and said, "Because you are one of mine, I will give you any wish. Be careful what you choose, however, because I will give your competitor twice whatever you ask for."

The grocer thought carefully about this wonderful opportunity, but every time he made a choice he remembered the condition: his neighbor would receive the same thing twice. If he asked for a large shipment of groceries, his rival would receive twice the shipment. If he asked for a new truck, his opponent would get two. This was not an easy choice. Finally, he arrived at a decision: "God, take away one of my eyes."

"Living by the soul" can lead to such foolishness as we deny the wisdom of the spirit, elevate ourselves and depend upon a blurred self-consciousness. Yet, the exaltation of knowledge in the soul radiates throughout the human cultural experience. One of its many ramifications is what has come to be called "world view."[96]

## WORLD VIEW:

## THE HEART OF OUR CULTURAL IDENTITIES

When the challenge of Kingdom personality was replaced with Satan-instigated human plans for cultural personality, problems mounted. By dismissing the principle of LIFE leading to KNOWLEDGE and initiating the new principle that knowledge could lead to life, new demands were placed upon humanity. By refuting God's principle, LIFE could no longer be the model and basis of human holiness; another ideal seemed necessary. The intimate personal sharing of LIFE as a prerequisite for the sharing of

KNOWLEDGE was replaced by a sharing of human knowledge so that there could be a sharing of life. Now, knowledge had to somehow animate life, instead of LIFE animating KNOWLEDGE. Love, as well as joy, freedom, and hope had to be redefined. Knowledge had to make a difference, now, because LIFE as God intended could no longer do so. The knowledge of good and evil now depended on human experience, lacking the measuring rod of God's LIFE, the benefit of his appraisal of right and wrong. These are the problems brought on by the choice of cultural personalities over Kingdom personality.

Summarizing the challenges rising from the choice of Adam and Eve to eat from the Tree of Knowledge of Good and Evil, we note that humanity was now required to . . .

- ✓ create a model of life
- ✓ provide a basis for living in cultural ways
- ✓ agree upon a shared understanding of life animating our living
- ✓ define and classify relationships and categories of life
- ✓ explain events and make adjustments
- ✓ rationalize contradictions, and
- ✓ arrive at distinct perspectives setting them apart from other groping humans.

All these challenges require an ordering of knowledge. When God's order was denied, another order had to be devised. When God's centrality was contravened, a new centrality emerged. Humanity at the center assigned God to a lesser position as God's perspective was rejected and humankind implemented a new perspective. World view is the result (See Figure 2 and note God's displacement to the realm of religion). All this ordering of knowledge is what world view is about. Christian anthropologist, Charles H. Kraft defines it as ". . . the central systematization of conceptions of reality to which the members of the culture assent (largely unconsciously) and from which stems their value system.[97] Kraft goes on to say that world view lies at the very heart of culture, "touching, interacting with, and strongly influencing every other aspect."

A common North American assumption, for example, links the self and independence.[98] Relating this supposition to each of the new requirements brought about by Adam and Eve's choice illustrates the centrality of world view in self-identity. America's *model of life* is

**When God's order was denied, another order had to be devised.**

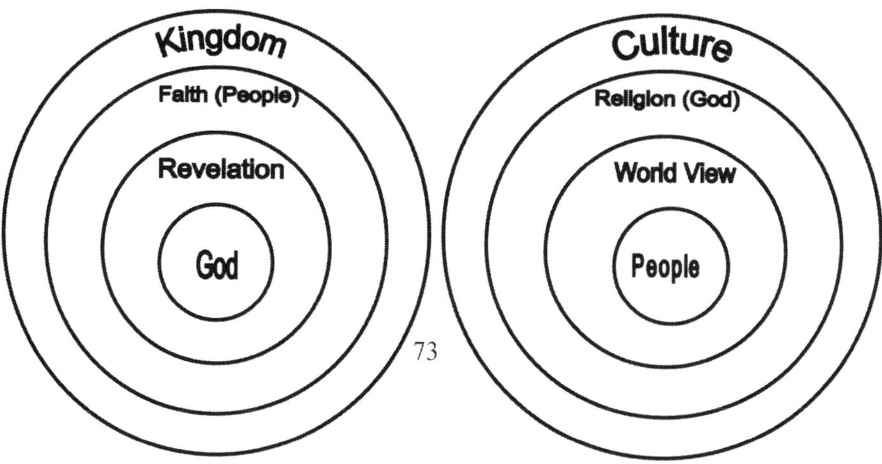


*Figure 2. Two Contrasting Perspectives.*

the rugged individualist who makes his or her own way *in cultural matters.* This independent self *lives according to relationships and categories of life* defined by society which emphasizes sex, role and achievements over family, residence and group. When a person gets into trouble, *events are often explained* in terms of the same assumption–"it's his own fault"–and the individual suffers from his own decision-making obligations. *Adjustments* require further decisions pursued personally.

The common theme of many North American movies deals with the consequences of this assumed linkage of self and independence. A person gets into a desperate situation (a kidnapping, blackmail threat or similar danger) and tries to escape without the help of family or authorities. All kinds of violence ensues as the hero or heroine wrestles with the *contradictions of their predicament* but hold *subconsciously* to the assumption. They *arrive at distinct perspectives* that lead into all kinds of predicaments totally removed from those of *other groping human beings.* A mall can be riddled with bullets, twenty cars wrecked in a mad chase across town and several lives lost. The assumption sticks like superglue and the movie ends with the star walking off alone.

## THE ORIGIN OF WORLD VIEW IDENTITIES

Such world view assumptions, like other aspects of cultural patterns, have their origins in the events of Genesis Three. Adam and Eve expressed this perspective first in the human experience, and then consistent with such conception of reality, responded religiously. As soon as the first man and woman ate the forbidden fruit, Genesis 3:7 says, "the eyes of both of them were opened, and they realized that they were naked; so they sewed fig leaves together and made coverings for themselves." They began to see in ways they had never seen before. Previous awareness of each other and their world based on God's revealed KNOWLEDGE had led to their understanding of companionship, covenant relationship, creation. Now, awareness led to feelings of fear, vulnerability, judgment and competition with each other.

Two new factors invaded the human situation. First, they replaced God-centeredness with human-centeredness. Previously they had seen the world according to God's perspective, revealed according to his will.[99] The Creator had been the source of their knowledge, revealing KNOWLEDGE unlike anything known to humanity since. There had been harmony between God's explanations of his creation and their observations of the same. The very language they spoke, the channel of perspective and revelation originating with God, had contributed to that harmony in God-empowered ways. Replacing God-centered KNOWLEDGE with their new and limited human-centered abilities, they now saw the world according to their human perspective, a vision consistent with world view. From this new center, humanity now perceived and judged life on the basis of knowledge. Now interpreted in human instead of divine ways, creation's purpose and plan were distorted in human misunderstanding and contradiction. God still loved and cared for them, but God's thoughts and ways were no longer open to them as they had once been.

Moreover, the new orientation toward the world and each other comprised not just one world view but two. Adam experienced the development of his world view; Eve experienced hers. The former harmony and unity between the two of them disappeared. Disharmony, misunderstanding and disorder began to rule between their personalities. Since then there has emerged, "A world with as many centers as there are human beings."[100]To simplify life and survive its unpredictable nuances, humans have had to band together and somehow agree on common world views. At the heart of every culture, these competitive views still struggle with the prevalent experience of humanity.

**Adam and Eve now saw the world according to their human perspective, a vision consistent with world view.**

World view contrasts have intrigued me for years. As an American living in Africa the contrasts become fascinating. I operate as a lone individual among people who see themselves primarily in terms of group identity. Disharmony and disorder occur when my world view assumptions about myself conflict with their assumptions about themselves.

For example, in a work situation, I find fulfillment in personal achievements. African colleagues find fulfillment in social relatedness. My office is defined by my accumulated books, the certificates and degrees hanging on my walls and files containing the collections of the past. The office of an African colleague may very likely contain the barest of books and achievement records but may be constantly filled with real people. Our work behaviors also reflect our world view assumptions about ourselves.

Linked to this are conflicting views of time, an important element of all world views. Time for me is point-oriented, for the people in my office it is event-oriented. A job begins and ends at certain points in time for me. It is an event for my African colleagues, the end-point (or deadline) not being that important. Conflicts follow when we allow world views to dominate our attitudes.

When Adam and Eve ate the fruit of the forbidden tree, a second factor intruded into their experience and ours, namely: religion. Religion and value systems stem from world view.[101] For example, if I assume that personal achievement is necessary to my self-identity, my religious beliefs and themes will most likely reflect the assumption. A church providing upward mobility may seem more enticing than one preaching the truth. On the other hand, if my assumption is that social relatedness is the main criterion for my identity, might I not seek a church that is close-knit and caring?

**Religion and value systems stem from world view.**

Remarkably, the first thing Adam and Eve did independently after eating from the Tree of Knowledge was make a moral judgment–a determination of right and wrong. They were suddenly ashamed of their own nakedness. Self-identity and self-expression took on new significance. In their sudden shame was planted the first seeds of disharmony in world view and religious orientation, soon to grow into a jungle of fear and suspicion.

God's revealed KNOWLEDGE had offered harmonious, loving relationships. Now the love intended by God stood forever skewed by the self-centered seeing experienced by both Adam and Eve rather than a God-centered perspective. Each wished "to make

**In their shame was planted the first seeds of disharmony in world view and religious orientation.**

the other his or her creature," says Genesis commentator Henri Blocher.[102] Each became an object for the other to dominate, use, manipulate, and from whom to extract favor. The "good" perceived by each now emerged as a rival good, not a united one. The independence of each became a reciprocal threat.

Significantly, when Adam and Eve first "see" in this way, they make themselves coverings of fig leaves. They try to cover their nakedness, suddenly so vulnerable, attempting to "evade the aggressive or seductive look, which seeks to captivate and to capture."[103] This is, I believe, the first cultural-religious behavior recorded in Scripture. Adam and Eve make their first moral judgment outside the counsel of God.

When Adam and Eve refused an identity grounded first in God, they became preoccupied with self-identities based on experiential knowledge creating and reinforcing competing world views. The emergent cultural personalities have fascinated observers ever since. Mars, Venus, Jupiter, Mercury–all are from the same galaxy and planetary system, but great distances exist between them. In like manner, humans try to cross great distances between each other in all kinds of global issues; elusive commonalties and stark differences make the journey a constant challenge. Religion, world view, cultural personality, life, knowledge, the presence of evil, and cultures themselves are part of the terrain.

The journey becomes a requirement for cross-cultural workers and Genesis Three shows Christians how these elements are allowed by the Creator, but not without serious limitations. The next chapter presents the challenges we face.

## FOR FURTHER STUDY AND DISCUSSION

1. *Use Table 1 to describe your own personality before becoming a Christian. Perhaps you can even show God's position in your cultural experience.*
2. *Have you received God's LIFE into your life? Can you describe some of the changes by reference to the Kingdom personality of Table 1?*
3. *How do you understand "soul" and "spirit" in human personality? Does linkage of cultures to the former and the Kingdom to the latter appeal to you? Why or why not?*
4. *Why was humanity compelled to respond to each of the challenges rising out of Adam and Eve's choice?*
5. *Figure 2 shows the new order created by Adam and Eve on the left. Note God's position in the realm of religion instead of at the center. How do you see this pattern expressed in societies of interest to you?*
6. *Chapter Nine will show how God maintains his eternal plan right in the midst of our temporal plans. Kingdom is not detached from culture as Figure 2 may imply. What are the consequences of such detachment? Do some Christians advocate such detachment? Discuss.*

## Chapter 7

# THE LIMITS OF OUR CULTURAL EFFORTS

Like a kaleidoscope accidentally dropped, its many-colored components scattering across the floor, cultures sometimes fall apart. Where I live, in a volatile part of the world, this is common. The cruelties of domination, war, famine, disease, epidemics, police states, military oppression, violence, lawlessness, corruption and poverty crush known patterns of living.

George Kinoti, an outspoken Christian scholar in Kenya notes that 33% of Africa's people are malnourished, 27 of the 40 poorest nations in the world are found on this continent, 55% of the rural people are absolutely poor as are 70% of the urban population.[104] He goes on to show that the GNP for all of Africa's 550 million people is $150 billion, the same as for Belgium's 10 million people. Shattering age-old designs for living, this daily oppression upon the continent threatens and eventually smashes personal and public worlds to pieces. Boundaries collapse and adjustments wildly scatter brightly colored values, shards of belief, long-held traditions of family life and social institutions. The special shape of norms for living no longer has a home.

In my American home, many people watch the crises of Africa on television. Though far removed from these particular physical traumas, they too suffer the break-up of familiar patterns for living. Loose morals, lost values, fragmented families, broken marriages, rising costs, lavish lifestyles, evil pleasures, deadly drugs, greed for money–these cruelties tip the American kaleidoscope over the edge.

**Cruelties tip the American kaleidoscope over the edge.**

Columbine High School of Littleton, Colorado was on the news as I first wrote these words. Fifteen deaths among students and staff. Two students armed with sawed-off shotguns and homemade bombs did it all then took their own lives. Life over the edge. Life minus LIFE.

Many see cultures more positively. One such proponent writes,

> When I looked around at my neighbors in a Philippine community where I lived for several years, for example, I saw strong families. Warm hospitality. Lots of time lavished on children. Enduring loyalties. The ability to live graciously on little money. A heritage of economic freedom for women. Creativity in music.[105]

She went on to describe these patterns as gifts from God, evidence of the wisdom and knowledge that come from Jesus. Cultures do contain order, institutions, structures, beliefs and values for which we can thank God and upon which we can build. Balanced perspective <u>is</u> necessary but dangers demand caution. Are the patterns from God or should we look more astutely at the scenario?

Cultural enthusiasts are sometimes like the people taking off in a new plane brimming with the latest technology and the most luxurious of comforts. A voice comes over the plane's intercom, "Good morning, ladies and gentlemen. Welcome aboard this maiden flight. We are climbing to our planned cruising altitude of 40,000 feet. All the plane's systems are working perfectly and we expect to land at our destination on time. This plane is completely computerized and there is no pilot. Everything is guided and monitored by the computer. Sit back, relax and enjoy the flight. Nothing can go wrong . . . can go wrong . . . can go wrong."

Cultural pessimists, on the other hand, may be those who never fly.

Whether positive or negative in our judgment, critical or uncritical, a common question requires an answer: Why do cultures fall short of the ideals upon which they are based? Why does the good sought often materialize with a complementary portion of evil? New wealth in Africa and corruption. New technology in America and a lack of accompanying ethic. Peaceful harmony in the Philippines disrupted by domestic and community violence. A realistic look at life smashes into an idealistic one. By recognizing the limitations of human life without God's LIFE we may appreciate more the boundlessness of the eternal Kingdom.

Genesis Three answers the questions. Not only do cultures build upon the wrong assumption that increased knowledge will lead to improved life, they are also deliberately limited by God in their pursuit of this increase. Human knowledge comes with a price tag based on God's economy/plan.

**Why do cultures fall short of the ideals upon which they are based?**

## WHEN BROKEN RELATIONSHIP CONFINE EFFORTS

Relationships are the pillars of cultures, yet they are not what they ought to be. In Africa, brokenness happens when tribes, clans, economic classes and nations collide. In America, shattered lives occur within the most intimate of relations: wives and husbands, parents and children, friends. Reasons for the deficiency are found in Genesis Three. The sinful, rebellious events of this chapter gave rise to the first cultural patterns but also the first crashing of the kaleidoscope so new.

*First*, Satan enters the picture, bringing new dimensions to relationships on earth.[106] He had been given no place in the Garden by God, but Adam, supposedly in charge, allowed him entrance. He sought to bring the rebellion he engineered in heaven down to earth, frustrating the King and subverting the Kingdom. The subtlety of his presence in the new emerging order and his continuing impact through the centuries cannot be denied. By the time of the New Testament he is called "the god of this age", the "ruler of the Kingdom of the air", and "the prince of this world."[107] One reason relationships in our cultures are not ideal is because Satan stalks the earth.

**One reason relationships in our cultures are not ideal is because Satan stalks the earth.**

*Secondly*, the original relationship between God and people is broken as God's sovereignty is "denied, holiness outraged, veracity questioned, goodness doubted, word disbelieved, disobeyed, and love spurned," says Ruth Paxson.[108] Innocent relationship with the Creator could never again be the same. After eating the forbidden fruit gave them knowledge, Adam and Eve hid from the Lord.[109]

Today we still follow Adam and Eve's example, avoiding God's centrality, trying to evade his scrutiny, confining him to our religion and our pious notions. For too many Christians he belongs to Sunday events but not to those on Monday and the rest of the week. We engage in business but seek not his will. We enjoy social affairs and never give him a thought. As long as we hide from him, these other relationships in our cultures fall short of our highest hopes.

**Having displaced God from the center of their world, Adam and Eve each tried to move into that imposed vacancy.**

In Genesis Three, the *third relationship*–that between man and woman–also becomes a wounded one, recognizably damaged from generation to generation.[110] Having displaced God from the center of their world, Adam and Eve each tried to move into that "still point of the turning world." They each posed themselves as the new absolute authority, becoming face-to-face opponents where before they had been partners. Shame intrudes as men and women become aware of selfish desires, unsatisfied longings, the loss of true community.

What they experienced then is still experienced by every man and woman today as we reject God's sovereignty and collect self-made conflicts. Like them, we refuse the divine perspective uniting us and claim the locus, the "I am" of reference. The fundamental relationship of man and woman is skewed. What is the result? Marriage isn't what it could be. Exposing every weakness, every difference of opinion, it leaves each partner vulnerable–naked before the other. A preacher reminded an unhappy young bride that she had taken her husband for better or for worse. "Yes," she replied, "but he is worse that I took him for."

Unintended, broken and wounded relationships in cultures have their origins in the events of Genesis Three. A *fourth relationship* remains for consideration–that of enmity between God and Satan.

> So the Lord God said to the serpent (Satan), "Because you have done this, cursed are you above all the livestock and all the wild animals! You will crawl on your belly and you will eat dust all the days of your life. And I will put enmity between you and the woman, and between your offspring and hers; he will crush your head, and you will strike his heel."[111]

This enmity between God and Satan began long before creation. Beyond cultures, the cosmos is the arena of this conflict of vast dimensions. Satan rebelled in the timeless span before our beginning, yet creation and cultures were sucked into the conflict. Satan, envious of the significance of our beginning, our sojourn, and our ultimate ending, brings to earth the enmity between him and God, souring every possible relationship in the universe.

Satan, rebelling against angelic knowledge of the eternal Kingdom of God, opposed the priority given to humanity to be created in God's own image. He resisted the idea that God would maintain his plan for the image in the perfection of Jesus Christ. More than that, he resisted the prominence given to LIFE, God's desire to live in covenant with created humanity.

What happened to relationships? Why don't we get along the way we should? We can only answer these questions by observing the events of

Genesis Three. Our cultures, among other things, attempt to bring order to disordered relationships. The derangement, however, spreads like gangrene.

## WHY AREN'T THINGS BETTER?

– We would have been a family of seven, but we lost a baby . . .
– We were doing well but then a fire destroyed everything we owned . . .
– All was fine with our family but then our father lost his job.

Patterns of living in different environments are attempts to correct obstructions to life. As such, cultures are good, helpful, and necessary to the human situation, but the presence of obstructions should lead us to ask a question: How did such impediments begin?

Genesis Three provides necessary answers. I believe such disturbances are part of the curse God placed on Adam and Eve along with all their progeny up to today. Blessing was curtailed and conditioned because of sin; curse became part of the new human experience. This may sound very negative. However, the Bible always takes us through life, never around it, and in doing so, helps us to see why life isn't better.

**Patterns of living in different environments are attempts to correct obstructions to life.**

Take the trauma of birth, for example. How can it be explained? God's words in Genesis 3:16 cannot be overlooked:"I will greatly increase your pain in childbearing . . .." Cultures positively establish patterns and plans dealing with childbirth. The sanitized corridors of American hospitals as well as the natural surroundings of Africa reflect this effort. The endeavor, however, is always within the limits established by God. Miscarriages befall us, not because they are God's will but because they are part of a world remade with people at the center instead of God. Five hundred thousand women die every year in childbirth.

The environment is another area of cultural concern. Ecology was just as critical in the Garden of Eden as now. Genesis 3:17 bears upon these aspects of our cultures: "Cursed is the ground because of you . . . ". The earth as a place of discovery and delight becomes a place of drudgery and despair. Surprise gives way to survival, hope to hostility.

Adam and Eve found ways to live with the curse. Their actions established the foundations for the diverse cultural ways characteristic of our world today. Farmers struggle against soil erosion and depletion, herders graze livestock on scanty grasslands, gatherers fight insects and rodents. Destruction hits. We wonder why the environment for life can't be better.

Another question we ask is, "Why can't our labor patterns be more effective, fair, balanced, prosperous?" Some will say, "we do not treat one another well." True, but before our own rebellion stands the rebellion of Genesis 3 and its consequences in Genesis 3:19:". . . By the sweat of your brow you will eat your food until you return to the ground . . .". God placed the new labor of humanity under a curse, not a blessing. In cultures, humanity struggles to respond to this limitation but the outcome is never satisfactory. Yearning capacity easily exceeds earning capacity, especially in this day and age. Are we licked before we start? No. But the way ahead is God's way–even after we have tried all the others.

Humanity's struggle with life and death is precarious, consuming, and, in the end, inconclusive. Some have suggested that all cultures may best be explained in terms of our handling of death. Boris Pasternak's Dr. Zhivago says history is "the systematic work devoted to the solution of the enigma of death. That is why people write symphonies and why they discover mathematical infinities and electromagnetic waves . . .." Genesis 3:20-24 has a special message for this struggle. After the rebellion God prevented immortal life on his previous terms. He imposed limitations that we cannot overcome, despite our efforts. Death becomes a foe instead of the friend God intended, a battle with cruelty instead of an acceptance of charity, an end instead of a beginning.

Should we give up? That our efforts are obstinate is clear even with Adam's determined act in verse 20:"Adam named his wife Eve because she was the mother of all who live." Adam resolved to go on in spite of the curse. I am intrigued with his new name for the woman. Until this time he had called her "woman," a result of God's revelation. Now he called her, "Eve," not the result of God's LIFE but the source of human life. The pattern is still evidenced today: somehow we will survive the consequences and limitations brought by sin. We, too, obstinately plunge ahead, blind to God's better plan for human continuity and contentment.

The dissatisfaction lingers, however. Things are never as good as we would like.

## WHAT'S WRONG WITH THE SYSTEM?

Difficult relationships and recognizable limitations in various aspects of our cultures lead to the realization that there is something wrong with these patterns originating in the curses of Genesis Three. Their beginnings are in human-centered systems of knowledge instigated originally by Satan and multiplied in error ever since. Knowledge, revered in the belief that it will lead to the satisfaction of life needs, is overwhelmed by God's imposed limitations.

**Knowledge, revered in the belief that it will lead to the satisfaction of life needs, is overwhelmed by God's imposed limitations.**

We Americans, for example, elevate our own style of knowledge. In the realm of activity alone, this system is dominant. We need to get things done, to make up our own minds, solve our own problems, assume personal responsibility, determine reasonable explanations for events, recognize the rights of others, hurry, and separate work and play.[112] American cultural knowledge leads, we think, to "life, liberty and the pursuit of happiness." Forged by society and our own peculiar culture to fit into this mode as good citizens, we are dominated by our knowledge. Our general world view supports that knowledge with assumptions and presuppositions seldom questioned and carefully reinforced by the centrality of individualism with every American at the center. Indeed, our religious values, relationships and activities circulate around this knowledge.

However, throughout the American system we confront limitations imposed by God. Broken and wounded relationships hamper the American dream. Satan is active in his own ways. Pain and suffering are all too real. The environment is not perfect. Labor keeps changing. Death disrupts. The limits are too well-known. The system seems inadequate, an opinion voiced around the world as people face global issues. Is there hope in our future?

The final chapter of this book shows that the limits of our cultures frustrate neither the intent nor the love of our Creator. Good news awaits Christian effectiveness for confronting global issues. Cultures are neither the first nor last word. God's Kingdom is.

## FOR FURTHER STUDY AND DISCUSSION

1. *In a newspaper or news journal story identify a group of people whose familiar patterns of living have been disrupted. What were the aggravating circumstances?*
2. *It is said that if you put a frog in hot water it will jump out immediately. Put a frog in cold water, however, and gradually raise the heat and it will slowly boil to death. How do today's societies illustrate this lesson?*
3. *Identify some of the limitations you have experienced in your own life in regard to a) relationships and b) well-being.*
4. *How is "curse," understood in your society and how does that understanding influence your understanding of Genesis 3? Using a concordance, study this word in the Bible.*
5. *God is not opposed to knowledge but he does limit it. Do you agree or disagree?*
6. *How can an understanding of the Kingdom principle, LIFE leads to KNOWLEDGE, resolve the problem of poverty in the world? Of ethics in a technological society? Of other global issues?*
7. *Find the word "humility" in a concordance and look up several scriptures. Relate these scriptures to the place of humility in human life as presented in this chapter?*

# Part IV

# GENESIS AND THE GOSPEL OF LIFE

Chapter 8

# THE ENDURING KINGDOM PLAN OF GOD

To the powerlessness of limited human life, American, African, European or Asian, God's promise of unlimited LIFE provides the hope we seek today in the midst of all our global issues. Foreshadowed in Genesis 3:15, the ministry of Jesus is asserted when God tells Satan:

> And I will put enmity between you and the woman, and between your offspring and hers; he will crush your head, and you will strike his heel.

**God's promise of unlimited LIFE provides hope.**

Surprisingly, Genesis Three concludes in a way that brings us back to the relationship of God's Kingdom and our cultures, of LIFE and life. Here shines the hope–and promise: the plans of humanity are not forever separated from the plan of God. He does not leave us alone in our limitations.

Two events in Genesis 3:21-24 show the promise of God's eternal gospel dream.

## GOD UPHOLDS THE WAY OF *LIFE*

Adam asserted the human centrality common to all cultures when he named his wife Eve, the mother of all living. Thereafter they must have thought life would have to proceed from their own knowledge and experience. Maybe they thought they were now on their own. They had both expressed such thoughts when, upon realizing what it meant to be naked, they immediately sewed fig leaves for themselves.[113]

By itself, however, such assertive action does not solve the human situation nor change the eternal plan of God. Whether or not recognized by any of the generations since, it takes God's presence to be truly a man or woman; his LIFE is necessary for the completion of our lives.

God's loving response as recorded in Genesis 3:21 shows that his Kingdom intent continues. Complex human circumstances do not change God's plans. The account reads:

> The Lord God made garments of skin for Adam and his wife and clothed them.

Contrast these "garments of skin" with the "coverings of fig leaves" of Genesis 3:7. Man and woman made the coverings but God made the garments. The coverings of human innovation are hurried and temporary but the garments, products of God's plans, are deliberate and lasting. The difference is seen most remarkably in the Hebrew words: fig leaves are used to make *khagare,* the apron-like coverings, but skins are used to make *kethoneth*, the coats that covered from head to foot. *Khagare* symbolizes human desperation, *kethoneth*, divine determination to love, save and prepare us for the presence of his LIFE in our lives.

**Complex human circumstances do not change God's plans.**

*Kethoneth* is the same word used in Exodus 28 and Leviticus 8:1-9 to describe the high priestly robe of Aaron.[114] More than mere coverings, Adam and Eve's God-designed garments, like Aaron's robes, signal the nature of God's gospel dream, an eternal plan, a divine intention, a steadfast and loving resolve on the part of God, deliberate and highly significant. *Kethoneth* announces the insignia of royalty, a majestic plan and the Royal King himself, the ensign of the very Kingdom of God.

Both products point to plans of cosmic significance. Representing more than simple technology, the apron-like coverings are the first products of a human-centered lifestyle by which Adam and Eve, along with all their progeny to contemporary times, act on their own evaluation of global issues, rather than looking first to God's. I believe the fig leaf coverings point to the emergence of plans small and great which would soon engulf every aspect of human life on earth–though never adequately. Just as the fig leaves were part of a pattern for living in that environment, humanity has tirelessly searched for

**The fig leaves point to cultures, the garments to the Kingdom plan from before the beginning of time.**

other patterns throughout the world. The fig leaves point to cultures, now described in this chapter as our own *selected* patterns for living whether those of a group of Indians in South America, a collection of families in Africa, a particular people in Asia, or a mixed group in North America.

Meanwhile, God proceeds with his own eternal plans. He exchanges the man-made *khagare* of Adam and Eve for his *ketboneth*. Asserting his Kingdom intent and embracing eternity's gospel, he puts their cultural attempt based on new-found human knowledge in its rightful place, overshadowing their newly invented cultural values with Kingdom value and significance. Out of the counsel of his sovereign nature, God declares his glorious purpose for people by clothing them with robes symbolic of his desire to make them a royal priesthood in his Kingdom, LIFE-in-life people. I Peter 2:9 reinforces the idea:

> But you are a chosen people, a royal priesthood, a holy nation, a people belonging to God, that you may declare the praises of him who called you out of darkness into his wonderful light.

**_What shall Christians do?_ Consistently bear Kingdom LIFE into every cultural situation of life.**

In this loving act of God, a model and a pattern for Christian presence in all cultures is seen with God himself as the example. The pattern: consistent Kingdom introduction of LIFE to every cultural situation of life. Implementing this model and pattern is the distinct opportunity of every person who has come to know that Jesus himself implemented this Kingdom pattern as the LIFE-in-life Son of God. His method? Unreserved dependence on LIFE.

Salient to this model and pattern for resolving global issues is LIFE, whether seen in the Tree of LIFE or the cross of Jesus Christ.[115] Like a shining thread woven into the tapestry of revelation, the promise of LIFE unites Scripture from Genesis 1-3 and continuing on to the last pages of the Bible.

## GOD'S _LIFE_ WILL ENGAGE WITHHUMAN LIFE

The centrality of LIFE engaging with life in God's master-plan is seen again in Genesis 3:24 -

> After he drove the man out, he placed on the east side of the Garden of Eden cherubim and a flaming sword flashing back and forth to guard the way to the tree of LIFE.

God upheld the way to eternal LIFE when Adam and Eve sinned. More than just a pathway in the Garden, however, that preserved was this grand, eternal gospel plan–the gospel from before the beginning of time. Sin would not hinder the divine intention. Sinners would not be doomed to alienation from God forever. He guarded the way.

The Tree of LIFE was literally the centerpiece of the garden by God's intention and design. Its fruit was foundational to the relationship he sought. The LIFE it portrayed was his own glory and majesty. That tree held forth the principle by which God's Kingdom would be implemented among all people in all cultures: through LIFE they would have KNOWLEDGE.

Though rejected through Satan's nefarious deceits, God would maintain the simple way to LIFE with perfect continuity in his plan. He would preserve his intention in the midst of the everyday life of his consecrated creation. LIFE, divine LIFE in the lives of humanity, would be his central thrust and the basis of his will for all people. This, his eternal Kingdom plan from before the beginning, at the beginning, and far beyond the beginning is still God's central thrust today, his gospel to all generations. He established the plan, took the initiative, paid the price, set the example, and showed the way for the Kingdom and his LIFE to be brought back into every sphere of cultural life. LIFE will always engage with life, fulfilling God's eternal love, righteousness and will.

The possibilities are majestic. Listen to the words of Isaiah 46:9-13.

> Remember the former things, those of long ago;
> I am God and there is no other;
> I am God, and there is none like me.
> I make known the end from the beginning,
> from ancient times, what is still to come.
> I say: My purpose will stand,
> and I will do all that I please.
> From the east I summon a bird of prey;
> from a far-off land, a man to fulfill my purpose.
> What I have said, that I will bring about;
> What I have planned, that will I do.

The possibilities can be applied to the questions posed at the beginning of this book:

- ✓ How does a current Christian challenge for the "recovery of forgotten first things" affect Christian solutions to global issues?
- ✓ What is at stake in the "re-ordering of life priorities in our cultures"?
- ✓ How do today's "shifting perspectives" affect global issues?
- ✓ If Christians need to "rethink our Christian identities, to revision our faith and to reform our thought," as some say, where do we start?
- ✓ If "the search for a defining center is urgent in order to engage cultures with a coherent gospel," how shall we respond when the advocates themselves fail to develop vibrant, all-encompassing frameworks?
- ✓ How adequate are "new visions beyond yesterday's images"?
- ✓ How appropriate are new ventures that break from our frenzied activity hurtling in all directions?

The answers to these questions lie in what God has planned from before the beginning of time and what he has implemented in our times. The gospel in Genesis provides the starting place to realize those answers. The first things cannot be recovered without a recovery of God's LIFE and his kingdom plan. If we reorder the priorities of our life but the existing list has no reference to the gift of God's LIFE, then the new priorities will still be wrong. If we adjust to the shifting perspectives but only end up with another world view with people at the center, then we have missed the most important perspective we can have–the perspective of revelation. If Christians don't start from God's plan from before the beginning of time, then efforts to rethink their identities, revision their faith and reform their thought will be fruitless. If God is not at the center, then every new framework will be wrong. If the new visions and ventures are those of pumped up leaders and not the vision and mission of God, then we remain blind in a world of great global issues.

Our study of Genesis 1-3 has merely introduced the possibilities and provokes further thought. It has sought to inspire, stir emotions, and kindle hope. The specifics remain to be discovered in all cultures. Two possibilities capture our attention as Christians and the next two books in this series bring them forward for consideration.

When we understand how LIFE engages with life as God has always intended, religion as a solution to global issues becomes inadequate and faith becomes a noble challenge. Like many, we may now be tempted to think we must confront global issues with more religious fervor–organizations, institutions, leadership, communication, money and resources. We must "get more religion."

No, that is not the possibility projected by this study. Faith speaks more clearly to the global issues we face. It is the first possibility. This faith recognizes God at the center, his revelation authoritative, and the Kingdom plan as God's reason for our salvation and sanctification. It does not belong to a Christian world view or to a Christian religion.

The second book in this series, Kingdom Faith: Breaking through Religious Boundaries makes the argument. It continues the study of Genesis and steps into Genesis 4 in new ways. Cain and Abel did not each represent religion as so many think–a good one and a bad one. Only Cain represented religion. Abel represented faith, a totally different kind of response that has God at the center.

When we become a gospel people living by faith rather than religion, then we can go on to confront the global issues around us in new ways. The third book in this series, The Kingdom Mandate: Foundations for Transformational Stewardship, explains the gospel way by giving its entire attention to Genesis 1:28 –

> God blessed them and said to them, 'Be fruitful and increase in number; fill the earth and subdue it. Rule over the fish of the sea and the birds of the air and over every living creature that moves on the ground.'

Called "the cultural mandate" by many Christians with genuine concerns for global issues, this third book in the series of Kingdom perspectives calls this "the Kingdom Mandate" and explains why. The Kingdom Mandate is the second possibility.

This mandate surpasses all talk of cultural mandates, is far more significant in our response to global issues, is much larger in scope, and is specifically related to God's eternal gospel intent. The third book relates everything to God's eternal kingdom plan in the midst of temporal cultural plans.

What can happen when LIFE engages with life as God has always intended? How has that gospel intent affected you? How has God's LIFE in your life changed you forever? How has the one who designed you released your destiny? How has he realized the hope of his divine gospel dream for you? Do you need to yield to God the King with his Kingdom plan? How can God's gospel dream influence the global issues of your day whether at home, in your community, nation and world?

I urge you now to seek out books 2 and 3 in the series and look for biblical answers to these questions.

## FOR FURTHER STUDY AND DISCUSSION

1. *Identify biblical accounts showing that "complex human circumstances do not change God's plans." Can you think of contemporary events showing the same?*
2. *Consider the way Christ clothes us in righteousness today as an outworking of God's Kingdom ministry in Genesis 3:21. Can you connect the events? How?*
3. *Is it "unfair" to link today's cultural efforts to improve life with the fig leaf efforts of Adam and Eve? Why or why not?*
4. *In what ways can the gospel be summarized as God's eternal desire for his LIFE to dwell in human life? Does this clarify salvation for you? If so, how?*
5. *Give an example of how humans enslave themselves to a given culture and thereby violate the possibilities of LIFE-in-life.*
6. *Share with someone else how LIFE finally came into your life.*

# ENDNOTES

1 The original cover of the book, an artistic image created by my friend, Lynn Hansen, attempted to show a kaleidoscopic design with a burst of light behind it.
2 John 1:4
3 John 1:5
4 John 8:12
5 1 Peter 2:9
6 Jay M. Pasachoff, Journey Through the Universe, Saunders College Publishing, New York, 1992, p.1.
7 See Stephen Hawking, A Brief History of Time: From the Big Bang to Black Holes, Bantam Books, New York, 1988.
8 Hugh Ross, The Creator and the Cosmos, Navpress, Colorado Springs, 1993, pp.67 and 148.
9 2 Timothy 1:8-9.
10 Titus 1:1-2.
11 1 Peter 1:20.
12 John 17:5 and 24.
13 Ephesians 1:4, Titus 1:2, Revelation 13:8, 17:8.
14 Ephesians 1:5.
15 Ephesians 3:6,10.
16 Matthew 25:34.
17 See Colossians 1:16-20, John 1:3, 5:22, 17:6,9 and 24, Revelation 3:14, Hebrews 1:2-3, Ephesians 1:4, 3:11 and 1 Peter 1:20.
18 Ecclesiastes 3:11.
19 Quoted by S.G.F. Brandon, History, Time and Deity, Manchester University Press, New York, 1965, p.7.
20 I am indebted to Mrs. Lyn Lusi, then a graduate student of Daystar University of Nairobi, Kenya for this insight.
21 Erich Sauer, The Dawn of World Redemption, Paternoster Press, Exeter, 1964, p.22.
22 1 John 1:5 and Colossians 1:12.
23 Psalm 10:16.
24 Jeremiah 10:10.

25 1 Timothy 1:17.
26 Psalm 145:13.
27 Daniel 4:3
28 See Alva J. McClain, The Greatness of the Kingdom, Brethren Missionary Herald Books, Winona Lake, Indiana, 1959, pp.8-15. Also, Wendel Willis, editor, The Kingdom of God in 20th-Century Interpretation, Hendrickson Publishers, , Peabody, Massachusetts, 1987; Bruce Chilton, ed., The Kingdom of God, Fortress Press, Philadelphia, 1984, and Howard A. Snyder, Models of the Kingdom, Abingdon Press, Nashville, 1991.
29 2 Peter 3:8.
30 George E. Ladd, The Presence of the Future: The Eschatology of Biblical Realism, Wm. B. Eerdmans, Grand Rapids, 1974.
31 Psalm 66:7 and 103:9.
32 1 Thessalonians 2:12, 2 Timothy 4:18 and 2 Peter 1:11.
33 Beryl T. Adkins, et.al, Collins-Robert French-English, English-French Dictionary, 2nd Edition, Dictionaire's Le Robert, Paris, 1988 - " *raison d'état*–reason for being or existence" (Random House Dictionary, 2nd Ed., unabridged, 1983 and as "the justifying reason for the existence of something" in The New Lexicon Webster's Dictionary of the English Language, Vol.2, Lexicon Publications, Inc., New York, 1986, p.826). The Kingdom can be seen not only as God's reason of state but also as our reason for existing. I describe it here as reason of state.
34 Jeremiah 29:11.
35 E. Stanley Jones, Is the Kingdom of God Realism? Abingdon-Cokesbury Press, New York, 1940.
36 Proverbs 8:22-23.
37 Erich Sauer, The Dawn of World Redemption, Paternoster Press, Exeter, 1964, p.15.
38 Psalm 33:9 and Jeremiah 10:12.
39 John 1:1-14 and Colossians 1:15-18.
40 Howard Snyder, Community of the King, 1977, also see his other volumes, Liberating the Church, 1983, The Problem of Wineskins, 1984, A Kingdom Manifesto: Calling the Church to Live Under God's Reign, 1985, Intervarsity Press, Illinois. My profit from Snyder's insights is applied in my own way and I don't mean to imply exact correspondence in our views.
41 Howard Snyder, A Kingdom Manifesto: Calling the Church to Live Under God's Reign, InterVarsity Press, Illinois, 1985, p.17.
42 1 Corinthians 2:6-7.
43 Ephesians 3:9.
44 Philip Crowe, "The God Who Speaks," *In* Bible Characters and Doctrines, Scripture Union, London, 1971, p.49.
45 Ray Stedman, Understanding Man, Word Books, Waco, Texas, 1975, p.25.
46 J. H. Bavinck says "There is always a Trinity in love, "he who loves, that loved, and love itself." The Impact of Christianity on the Non-Christian World, Wm. B. Eerdmans, Grand Rapids, 1951, p.326.

47 Henri Blocher, In the Beginning: The Opening Chapters of Genesis, (Translated by David G. Peterson), InterVarsity Press, Illinois, 1984, p.81.
48 David Hocking first brought this to my attention in one of 1970s radio messages.
49 1 Peter 1:12, Romans 8:19.
50 Eugene Nida, God's Word in Man's Language, n.d., p.66.
51 Emil Brunner, Man in Revolt, 1939, Westminster Press, pp.109-110, Philadelphia. For other explanations, see G.C. Berkouwer, Man: The Image of God, Wm. B. Eerdmans, Grand Rapids, 1962; D.J.A. Clines, The Image of God in Man, Tyndale House, Philadelphia, 1967; Philip E. Hughes, The True Image: The Origin and Destiny of Man In Christ, Wm. B. Eerdmans, Grand Rapids, 1962.
52 See David J. Hesselgrave, Communicating Christ Cross-culturally, Zondervan Publishing House, Grand Rapids, 1978, for an excellent discussion of the differences.
53 Matthew 6:33.
54 John Mbiti, African Religions and Philosophy, Heinemann, London, 1969, pp.108-109
55 Genesis 2:9, 16, 3:22.
56 Revelation 22:2,19.
57 John 5:26.
58 See, for example, Erick Sauer, The Dawn of World Redemption, The Paternoster Press, London, 1951, p.95.
59 Genesis 2:8,9.
60 DeVern F. Froneke, The Ultimate Intention, Sure Foundation, Cloverdale, Illinois, 1963, pp. 60-61. This seemingly forgotten apologist of 50 years ago pinpoints a truth seldom considered by others trapped in traditional theological formulations that have more to do with human loyalties than divine authority.
61 1 Corinthians 15:45-46.
62 Erich Sauer, The King of the Earth, The Paternoster Press, London, 1962, p.82, says the same. The clear understanding of life and LIFE, Culture and Kingdom is missing from his assessment, however. Concerns other than those of this book prompted his study.
63 Emil Brunner, Man in Revolt, Westminster Press, Philadelphia, 1939, p.97.
64 W. Ian Thomas, The Mystery of Godliness, Pickering and Inglis Ltd., London, 1964, p.56.
65 Psalm 8:1-9.
66 Ephesians 2:10.
67 See Ruth Paxson's section on the human spirit in Life on the Highest Plane, Moody Press, Chicago, 1926.
68 Hans Walter Wolff, Anthropology of the Old Testament, Fortress Press, Philadelphia, 1974.
69 John 4:24.
70 Matthew 5:14.
71 Romans 8:16.
72 Charles Wesley, "And Can It Be That I Should Gain," Hymns for the Family of God, Paragon Associates, Inc., Nashville, Tennessee, 1976, p.260.

73 W. Ian Thomas, The Saving Life of Christ, Zondervan, Grand Rapids, 1961. Thomas's attention to this principle was revolutionary in my life. Though seemingly absent elsewhere in the literature, I believe he struck biblical gold on this subject. My additions are in the realm of the Kingdom as God's eternal plan and our own cultural designs.

74 John 17:3.

75 See William A. Dyrness' The Earth is God's: A Theology of American Culture (1997, Oribis Books, Maryknoll, New York, pp.81-84) for a good description of the resultant "culture wars" raging in the USA. Note, however, that Dyrness' solutions show no comprehension of LIFE as described in this book.

76 A.L. Kroeber and Clyde Kluckhohn, Culture: A Critical Review of Concepts and Definitions, Vintage Books, New York, 1963, p.3.

77 James P. Spradley and David W. McCurdy, Anthropology: The Cultural Perspective, Alfred A. Knopf, New York, 1975, p.2.

78 Op.cit., pp.9-16.

79 Marvin Mayers and Stephen Grunlan, Cultural Anthropology: A Christian Perspective, Zondervan, Academie Books, Grand Rapids, 1979, p.39

80 1 Corinthians 10:10, Revelation 12:9-10.

81 Ruth Paxson, Life on the Highest Plane, Moody Press, Chicago, 1926, p.70. Mark I. Bubeck, in his book, The Adversary: The Christian Versus Demon Activity, Moody Press, Chicago, 1975, misses this description of Satan, emphasizing, like most, his evil ways. Paul's warning in 2 Corinthians 11:14-15, where Satan is seen as one masquerading as an angel of light, receives minimal attention. Bubeck misses the most subtle of Satan's ways.

82 Lewis Sperry Chafer, Satan, His Motive and Methods, Zondervan Publishing Co., Grand Rapids, 1919, pp.73-74.

83 Op.cit., pp.75-76.

84 Douglas D. Webster, Christian Living in a Pagan Culture, Tyndale Publishers, Wheaton, 1980, p.154.

85 W. Ian Thomas, The Mystery of Godliness, Pickering and Inglis Ltd., London, 1960, p.50.

86 Op. cit. pp.79-80.

87 Sherwood Lingenfelter, Transforming Culture: A Challenge for Christian Mission, Baker Book House, Grand Rapids, 1992, p.17.

88 Lingenfelter shared these insights at an SIL Anthropology Workshop held at Brackenhurst Conference Centre, Limuru, Kenya, June, 1997.

89 John Gray, Men Are from Mars, Women Are from Venus, HarperCollins Publishers, New York, 1992, p.5.

90 See Eugene Nida, Custom and Culture, Harper and Brothers, New York, 1954, pp.16-17, for captivating discussion of such differences.

91 Genesis 3:6.

92 Strong's Concise Dictionary of the Words in the Hebrew Bible, n.d., p.62, article 3045.

93 Ruth Paxson, Life on the Highest Plane, Moody Press, Chicago, 1926, p.26.

94 Watchman Nee, The Normal Christian Life, Victory Press, London, 1957, pp.152-153.

95 Watchman Nee, The Spiritual Man, Christian Fellowship Publishing, Inc., Hollis, New York, 1978, pp.47-48.

96 While many prefer to make this one word–worldview, I prefer two words. Among other things, our world views contrast with God's view–a contrast seen more clearly with the use of two words.

97 Charles H. Kraft, Christianity in Culture: A Study in Dynamic Biblical Theologizing in Cross-cultural Perspective, Orbis Books, Maryknoll, 1979, p.53. Kraft writes on the subject as a Christian anthropologist. Others write from a Christian philosophical view point: Arthur F. Holmes, Contours of a World View, Wm. B. Eerdmans, Grand Rapids, 1983; James W. Sire, Discipleship of the Mind, InterVarsity Press, Downer's Grove, Illinois, 1990.

98 Edward C. Stewart, American Cultural Patterns: A Cross-cultural Perspective, Intercultural Network, Inc., LaGrange Park, Illinois, 1972, p.62.

99 Deuteronomy 29:29.

100 Emil Brunner, Man in Revolt: A Christian Anthropology, Westminster Press, Philadelphia, 1939, p.9. Sigmund Freud bore this out with his query, "What do women want?" A recent study of the different worlds of men and women is John Gray's Men Are from Mars, Women Are from Venus, Harper-Collins Publishers, New York, 1992. See Note 1.

101 Charles H. Kraft, Christianity in Culture: A Study in Dynamic Biblical Theologizing in Cross-cultural Perspective, Orbis Books, Maryknoll, 1979, p.53.

102 Henri Blocher, In the Beginning: The Opening Chapters of Genesis, InterVarsity Press, Illinois, 1984, p.173.

103 Op.cit., p.174.

104 George Kinoti, Hope for Africa and What the Christian Can Do, AISRED, Nairobi, Kenya, 1994. His observations are twenty years old. What are the conditions today, twenty years later? 1) The percentage of Africa's people who are malnourished is still at 32%; 2) 34 of the top 40 poorest countries in the world are in Africa–that is 34 out of 45 countries, seven more than in 1994; 3) absolute poverty (at $1 per day) is the condition of 31% of Africa's rural population and 16% of its urban population–seemingly, an improvement; 4) Africa's population today is at 1.1 billion–it has more than doubled in 20 years; 5) the GDP for Africa is $2,579 while in Europe as a whole it is $32,471; Africa's GNP has almost doubled to $284 billion a year but Belgium's quadrupled to $483 billion.

105 Miriam Adeney, "Culture and Planned Change," pp. 135-177, in The Church in Response to Human Need, Samuel Vinay, Editor, Eerdmans, Grand Rapids, 1983

106 Genesis 3:1-7.

107 2 Corinthians 4:4, Ephesians 2:2, John 12:31.

108 Ruth Paxson, Life on the Highest Plane, Moody Press, Chicago, 1918, p.95.

109 Genesis 3:8-11.

110 Genesis 3:12-13.

111 Genesis 3:14-15.

112 See books like Edward C. Stewart and Milton J. Bennett's American Cultural Patterns: A Cross-Cultural Perspective (Intercultural Press, Yarmouth, Maine, 1992 ) for a full discussion of American lifestyles.

113 Genesis 3:7.

114 I first learned this from M.R. DeHaan, Portraits of Christ in Genesis, Zondervan Publishing, Grand Rapids, 1960, p.70. See also James Strong, Strong's Exhaustive Concordance of the Bible, World Bible Publishers Madison, New Jersey, 1992 (from the 1890 original). Strong uses the King James Version and thus refers to "coats of skin." He describes *kethoneth* under article 3801 in the Hebrew and Chaldee Dictionary of the Old Testament, p.76. *Meheel* (article 4598, p.91) is another word also used for the high priestly robe of Aaron.

115 John 10:10.

**OTHER BOOKS BY LARRY L. NIEMEYER AND AVAILABLE FROM AMAZON.COM.**

The gospel has been made to be many things: part of the Christian religion, an important piece in a complex religious system, a message controlled by religious specialists, a subject to be studied in religious institutions, a writer's topic.

This book presents a simple biblical argument for the gospel as God's dream from before the beginning of time. That dream: that His LIFE would dwell in human life through Jesus Christ. Thus, his dream endures into all eternity while ours dissipate and disappear.

The thirty years Jesus lived on earth fulfilled God's eternal gospel dream to bring eternal LIFE to every human life that accepted his own LIFE-in-life presence as Son of God.

The Apostle John did not get that message at first although he walked with Jesus for three years. The resurrection changed all that. Then he spent the rest of his life walking like Jesus, a LIFE-in-life man.

We resemble John. Satisfied to walk with Jesus somehow, we fail to walk like Jesus as he desired–as LIFE-in-life people, believing, but also living out the gospel.

**BE ON THE LOOKOUT FOR OTHER BOOKS BY LARRY L. NIEMEYER AND SOON AVAILABLE FROM AMAZON.COM.**

Kingdom Faith: Breaking through Religious Boundaries

The Kingdom Mandate: Foundations for Transformational Stewardship

Cultural Studies for LIFE-in-Life Service in Africa

Field Tools for Building LIFE-in-life Relationships in Africa

Exploring Deep Culture for Transformational LIFE-in-life Service in Africa

Discipleship Mobilization: A Kingdom Necessity in the African City

Contacts:
E-mail: larry@harvest21.org
Website: http://www.harvest21.org

Made in the USA
San Bernardino, CA
22 January 2014